UNCHAINED

A Journey from Abuse to Inspiration

UNCHAINED

A Journey from Abuse to Inspiration

Mike Nunnally

Unchained: A Journey from Abuse to Inspiration / Mike Nunnally
ISBN: 979-8-863-09384-0

DEDICATION

God has always protected me and placed Angels in my path to help guide me along the way.

This book is dedicated to all those Angels, and to those friends, students, ballplayers, campers, and counselors who have supported me and enriched my life by their presence!

And of course to my family, who continues to be my strength and shield!

God bless you all!

Don't give up. Don't give in.

—Mike Nunnally, life motto

CONTENTS

FOREWORD

If you could be transported to the open-air, stone chapel in Orkney Springs, Virginia, during the summers of the middle and late 1980s, you would hear hundreds of teen and pre-teen campers and their counselors strumming guitars and singing their hearts out in surprisingly-tight harmonies. The songs rise up from the Cathedral Shrine of the Transfiguration and echo through the mountain forest.

One of the lead voices is the director of the St. George's Camp. Some call him "Mike." Others call him "Chief." Hundreds of athletes and students in the valleys beyond call him "Coach." He is my friend, Mike Nunnally, and his life story is a saga of transfiguration, of transformation.

Now and then we meet persons who have a certain aura. They radiate an atmosphere of confidence, yet leave us free from pressure. They express their opinions, but we feel no compulsion to agree. These people are not cold or aloof. It's simply that they are so solid that they want nothing from us but that which we can give freely. Those singing youngsters and counselors felt safe, could be themselves, could flourish and grow. Individuals like Mike have the power to convey a most extraordinary gift.

But most of those campers, counselors, athletes, and students did not know all of his life story. They didn't realize that their compassionate leader, who was singing so boldly, had lived a life that traced an arc of dramatic change. His was a soul scrubbing journey: through pain and loneliness, abuse, abandonment … and eventually of hope, rescue, brotherhood, support, and affirming growth.

And so, with this book, Mike has given us another extraordinary gift. We need to hear stories like this. You will be a better person for walking with him through these pages.

The Rev. Roger Bowen,
Staunton, Virginia, Fall 2023.

ACKNOWLEDGMENTS

It has taken a lot of support and encouragement for me to put my life into words. For many years my children, Pete and Brooke, listened to stories of my youth and asked me to write down the stories I would tell them.

Once I started writing and let my sister, Celia, look at my early efforts, she would text me daily and ask for "more pages." That spurred me on when I sometimes didn't feel like putting in the effort.

My editor, Mary Sproles Martin, did an excellent job with her skills and advice for a novice author. She helped me keep my voice on the pages.

Rekha Kaula showed her creativity and expertise in designing a book cover dealing with tough subject matter.

INTRODUCTION

This is the story of an abused, troubled, twelve-year-old boy who was taken from his mother and stepfather and placed in a home for boys from 1956–1963.

How did it come to this, and what happened to this boy going forward? Who were the people and what were the themes and experiences that—against all odds—helped shape him and turn him into a functioning member of society?

This is the story of a boy who escaped his beleaguered past to become a husband, father, church leader, and Christian summer camp director. A boy who grew into a man who spent thirty-plus years teaching and coaching, impacting thousands of lives in a positive way.

That boy is me, and these are my stories of faith, love, brotherhood, compassion, transformation, and resilience.

SECTION ONE
NORFOLK

Unchained

1

FREE AT LAST

The detectives took the key to the lock from my mother and unlocked the chain from my leg. The chain was on so tight that it caused chafing and bruising and I couldn't get my fingers between it and my skin. The officers were very upset with my mother and asked her how a mother could be a part of something like this. She looked dazed and confused, and really had no answer for them.

They had knocked on the door of our house that Saturday afternoon, July 7, 1956. I was twelve years old. They couldn't believe what they saw when they identified themselves and I let them in. I was standing in the hallway, holding one end of a five-foot chain. The other end was locked around my right ankle.

Chris Cheek, my stepfather, was a sick man. The chain was just another way he had devised to punish me. In addition to being physical punishment, the chain would keep me from going outside and playing with the kids whose parents had turned him in to the police for abusing me. He left for work for the Norfolk and Western Railroad about three-thirty p.m. Just before leaving, he would lock the chain on my leg and take the key with him. My mother also had a key to the lock, and when she got home from her job as a waitress between eight-thirty and nine o'clock at night, she would unlock the chain, and I could take it off my leg.

Because he didn't lock the other end of the chain to anything else, just the one end to my ankle, I had mobility around the house. The chain wasn't heavy. It was the one we used to walk our very large Scottish Deer Hound. I just had to carry it in one hand whenever I moved from one place in the house to another. I often thought of taking that chain and wrapping it around my stepfather's neck!

Chris Cheek was wrong about me not being able to go outside with the chain on, though. I had been out on the porch earlier that day and a passerby had seen me with the chain on my leg and called the police.

I explained the locking and unlocking routine to the detectives as they drove me to Bell's Seafood Restaurant in downtown Norfolk, Virginia, where my mother worked. At the same time, another police car was dispatched to arrest my stepfather.

The detectives kept the chain, lock, and key for evidence, but before they took me to the Juvenile Center for the weekend, they took me back to the police station for a reenactment picture. They apologized profusely and asked me to put the lock and chain on my leg for the photographer. They had me cover my face with my left hand as he snapped the picture. I found out many years later that the picture and an accompanying article about my stepfather's arrest had appeared in the local newspaper's Sunday edition the next day. I was famous and didn't know it!

I have often thought about the question the detective had angrily asked my mother. How could she be a part of chaining her son?

Sometimes we go along in life and things get slowly out of hand. Before we know it, the situation has overwhelmed us. It's so hard to change course, and, over time, we accept the unthinkable as the norm. If we were able to see in the beginning where we would be in the end, there is no way we would have traveled that path.

For so many of us, it's very hard to extricate ourselves from a situation that has quietly overtaken our lives. We become too comfortable with the way things are, even when we know in our hearts it is wrong. We find excuses and ways to justify our behavior, because to change would take a dramatic shift in our life's path, often accompanied by uncertainty and emotional pain. I think a lot of that is what happened with my mother. She let herself get caught in a situation that she couldn't control, and in the end, it cost her dearly.

After the picture for the newspaper was taken at the police station, I walked out, got in the police car, and we headed for the juvenile center for boys. I thought to myself, I am free! Since it was a weekend, the detectives took me to the juvenile center until Social Services could find a placement for me. I asked the detectives to put the flashing lights and the sirens on, drive fast, and turn the radio on real loud to a rock-and-roll station. They were more than happy to oblige, and we sang what are now "oldies" at the top of our lungs! We even stopped for candy and a soda on the way. I was so happy that I would be spending a couple of nights there, and not at home. I asked the detectives if I would ever have to go back to my house, and they said, "Not a chance!"

I never saw my stepfather, Christopher Cheek, again. He was in my thoughts for years, however, mostly me just thinking of how I'd like to do him in. He helped shape my personality going forward though, as my time on 34th Street certainly played a big part in my social and emotional development. I didn't crawl into a little ball, become introverted and feel sorry for myself because of what had happened to me. Instead, I became outgoing, even happy go lucky on the outside, hiding my emotions in this way.

It was only years later that I was able to piece together the events that took place to bring my life to the screwed-up mess that I was in!

Our family moved to Norfolk from Georgia when I was five, and up until that point I really didn't know my mother, my sister, Celia, or my brother, Howell, very well. My father, Victor Nunnally, had split and left for New

Orleans when I was three, basically deserting his children. I don't remember him at all.

My sister and brother had been in children's homes, and I had been "boarded out" since I was a baby, because my mother said she couldn't support us. She had met Chris Cheek on a Greyhound bus in 1946 and he convinced her to move to Norfolk and get a job there. They married the next year and sent for us all, two years later, in 1949. For some reason I never did learn, my mother's own family had turned their back on her. This was unusual, for even in those hard times, families took care of their own.

Chris Cheek had no children of his own and didn't really have the disposition to be a parent. He certainly lacked the parenting skills necessary to raise a young boy who was full of life and energy. I don't think he ever hugged me or told me that he cared for me. It seemed like I was an aside in his life— someone he had to tolerate. I never developed any kind of relationship with him. His idea of parenting and of discipline was to ridicule and scorn, to dole out emotional abuse, his hand, the belt, both the leather, and occasionally, the buckle. Oh, and one other method: the chain.

He became the only person I have truly hated. I eventually came to see him as someone who had some kind of mental condition or illness.

It wasn't until much later that I found out what had happened to him. He was charged with child abuse on me for the second time, and this time knew he would be going to jail. He paid his bond, then skipped town and headed to Georgia with my mother. I used to revel in the fact that he spent the rest of his life as a criminal.

The detectives got me checked into the juvenile center and told the people in charge that I was a "special" resident, and that I was to be kept away from the other boys. Shortly after the detectives left, however, I started lobbying the guards there to at least let me go hang out by the ping pong tables.

One of them said he would stay with me for a while, so we went over to where the two tables were located. Both tables were occupied, and there were a few boys waiting to play.

Now in those days it went like this; game to twenty-one; winner stays until he loses. That's the way it had been at the Boys Club at the corner of Colonial Avenue and 27th Street, just a few blocks from my house. I had started going there when we lived closer to the club, and continued to go there when we moved to 34th Street. That's where I fell in love with ping pong, and where I spent many hours waiting and learning to play the game.

I was pretty good for my age when I picked up the paddle for my first game in the juvenile center. In those days, I played pretty much a defensive game, just trying to get the ball back over the net until my opponent made a mistake and hit the ball into the net or off the table. Over two hours later there was a crowd around my table. Evidently these boys had been spending too much of their time getting into trouble, and not enough time at the ping pong table. It was weird; they were all pulling for the little guy with the white hair!

I think the word had gotten out that I was "special," and maybe they found out why I was there. I'm not sure about that, but I realized for the first time how much I loved being in the spotlight in competition. The guards had to almost pry that paddle from my hand when it came time for lights out, and my "church" the next day, Sunday, was that table.

I left the detention center on Monday morning with a spring in my step, my first nickname, "Whitey," and with the knowledge that being good at games gave you a certain status among your peers. Boys Home of Virginia, (where I would live for the next seven years) had ping pong tables too! And a tournament every year. I'm not sure when I first won that tournament, but I know I was top dog in the ping pong department from at least my ninth grade year until I graduated.

Unchained

2

O Lamb of God, I Come, I Come

On Monday, when I left the detention center, I was taken to live with a foster parent family on a temporary basis. Social Services was searching for a permanent home for me. I immediately made a friend who was streetwise, and he asked, "You want to make some money?" Well, sure I did!

The foster parents' house was in the Ocean View part of town, with a golf course and an amusement park nearby. I can't remember the boy's name, so I'll call him Jimmy. Jimmy said we needed money for the amusement park, and he knew how to get it. I followed him around like a little puppy, and we ended up at the golf course, hunting for lost golf balls. Now here was something I found I was good at, and in no time, we had a dozen or so. I asked Jimmy what was next, and he said we are going to sell them to the golfers as they come by. Easy right? Not exactly Jimmy explained. We had to make sure the folks who worked at the golf course didn't see us, as our form of entrepreneurship was frowned upon. I was proud of myself over the next few days as we skirted the authorities, and I loved the feeling of the wind on my face riding the roller coaster! I thought that Jimmy, with his business sense, would do well for himself in the future.

I was placed with the Walker family. After a couple of days, I thought, "This is a nice normal, family." Etta was the mom, and we hit it off right away. I could not keep from smiling ear-to-ear when she said, "You're a part of our family now." Their son, Tommy, was fifteen or sixteen, and he was a stud! I looked up to him right away as he had it all going; good looking, great student, and he became an All-State running back who later attended VPI (now Virginia Tech) on a football scholarship. Their daughter's name was Joyce-Fay, and she was three years younger than me. We somehow decided we were going to argue and squabble a lot in the beginning! The other member of the family was a man I came to love and admire: Burley Walker.

Burley was a truck driver by trade and drove his eighteen-wheeler up and down the East Coast helping to provide for his family. He owned his truck, and as time went by, I found out that he was gone a lot, and that his truck was always needing to be fixed. He also didn't seem to be much of a talker. When I first went to stay with the Walkers, they were living in Broad Creek Village, a large group of temporary housing that had been built to help alleviate the housing shortage caused by World War II. It had been started in the early forties, and was pretty much a self-contained community with its own shopping, police, schools, fire department, etc. We were all getting used to each other and I had just started seventh grade, but something happened that made me think it was all going to fall apart.

I cried, and cried, and cried. I had been found out. I had been abusing the Walker's little dog, Tricksie, and one day I got caught. She was small and looked like a Jack Russell, but she would have been called "mutt" in those days.

Tricksie was small, so they took her everywhere with them, and they loved her dearly. When I lived on 34th Street with my mother and stepfather, we had two dogs, Blackfoot and Hippodrome (Hippy). They were great company for me, as I was alone on school nights from three-thirty to nine or nine-thirty. Tricksie, however, didn't take to me right away. I would call to her, and she wouldn't come, and if I tried to pet her, she would shy away. At first this just made me feel bad, but at some point I started feeling rejected and got mad about it. All I wanted was for Tricksie to love me, and I could not understand why she wouldn't.

When no one else was around I started hitting and kicking that poor dog. She would run from me and hide behind the furniture, especially the couch. I would sometimes take off my belt and hit her with it, and she would whimper. It wasn't too long before the Walkers realized something was wrong, as Tricksie would not get near me and shied away from me whenever I came into the room.

One day when no one else was around, Burley sat me on the couch and asked me if I had been hitting Tricksie. I was afraid to tell him the truth, so I lied through my teeth and said no. Then the floodgates opened, and I told him the truth. I cried and cried, sobbed, and sobbed. I couldn't stop shaking, I was so ashamed of myself.

Burley pulled me to him and put his big arms around me, holding me close to him. He said nothing as I cried myself out, just kept holding me and rocking me gently back and forth. I couldn't bring myself to even look at him, so he gently lifted my chin and looked me in the eyes. He said, "It's OK, Mike. I understand. I'm not mad at you." Of course, that just made me start crying all over again, and I held him so tight.

He knew that I was just acting out what I had experienced, that I had a lot pent up inside of me.

God put the Holy Spirit in Burley Walker that day, guiding his every thought, word, and action. Doing and saying just what I needed. It was as if God had held me in his arms, and was whispering to me, "It's OK, Mike. I understand." I never hit Tricksie again, and eventually we came to share a good relationship. The thing that stuck with me, though, was the fact that Burley never said another word about it; never let on that it happened. This was the first time in my life that I was treated that way, and it was a lesson learned. Burley taught me the value of forgiveness and showed me that even when we make mistakes, we can still be loved and accepted.

Saturday came and Etta said, "We need to take you and get some Sunday clothes because we are going to church tomorrow." Off we went, and my eyes got wide as I got my first glimpse of a shopping center. We walked into a nice store and Etta told the salesman to fit me with a nice suit, at a reasonable price. In a few minutes I was smiling and strutting around the store in my first-ever suit! I asked Mrs. Walker, "What about a pair of shoes? She laughed and said, "One thing at a time. Don't you have shoes on your feet?"

I woke up the next morning excited to be heading to church! A twelve-year-old boy excited about church? Yep. The Episcopal Church of the Ascension near my house had become a haven for me, a shelter from the storm. My sister, Celia, started taking me there with her when we moved north, and I continued to attend every Sunday after she and my brother, Howell, had both left the house. My mother and stepfather never went to church, and that was fine by me. The church also gave me an opportunity to do one of my favorite things. Sing! From an early age I would sing anywhere and everywhere.

The first song I can remember singing was *Good Night Irene*, which hit number one in 1950. That was the version recorded by the Weavers, but the original was sung by Huddie 'Lead Belly' Ledbetter in 1933. I can remember annoying my family by singing that song over and over—in the house, out on the street, everywhere! Another one of my favorites was *I'm Looking Over a Four-Leaf Clover*.

As we pulled into the parking lot, I noticed that Foxhall Baptist was a lot bigger than Ascension, and as we walked in to sit down, I thought, "This place is huge!" Three separate rows of pews formed a semi-circle toward the front. I took my cues from Etta on what to do when, and we started with a hymn right away. I didn't know it or any of the others during the service, I just picked them up as we went along.

I looked over at Etta and she was smiling at me as she sang. I smiled back. The service was fun but so much different from the Episcopal tradition. The biggest thing I noticed; no kneeling to pray! Just bow your head. That was easy. At the end of the service, the music started playing softly, folks swaying back and forth in time to the hymn, *Just As I Am*. I had never heard it before, but this hymn was to become very familiar to me as it was played at the end of almost every service.

Now this was something totally new to me, as the preacher started talking softly to the rhythm of the music, people just singing along when it was time for the refrain; "O Lamb of God, I Come, I Come." After a bit, I watched as some of the worshippers left their seats and started walking down the aisles toward the preacher, some with their arms lifted skyward.

When they got to the front, he would touch them gently and guide them to a spot near him but off to the side. This went on for several minutes as the music gently played, and the preacher continued to invite people to come forward to "give their life to Christ." When it was clear that the procession forward had stopped, the preacher would gather them all together and pray over them and welcome them into the faith.

This whole thing seemed very holy, somber, and sincere.

It was a different kind of worship, but I enjoyed it just the same, and as I walked out in my new Sunday clothes, I felt a sense of pride and belonging that I had never felt before.

During the vacation times I spent over the years with the Walkers, this scene played out on a regular basis. I never felt "called" in that way, and hoped God loved me anyway. Which proved out! Funny though, I could swear some of those folks came forward more than once as I continued to attend church.

Unchained

3

HERE COME THE JUDGE

One evening, Etta let me know Social Services was picking me up the next morning. As I got in their car after breakfast, I asked why they needed me, and the answer was that I was going for a pre-trial interview with the prosecutor's office, and they would be asking about my home life.

I smiled to myself and thought, "This is my big chance to put it all out there! Get back at Chris Cheek for all he had done to me!"

We hadn't sat down before I started with a litany of his abuses!

The interviewer told me to slow down and wait for his questions. It's too much to put it all down here, so I'll just summarize what I ended up telling him:

- It started when my sister and brother moved out, and he moved in.
- I was eight years old. As I got older, the punishments escalated.
- If I lied, I had to brush my teeth with detergent.
- If I soiled my underwear, I was forced to wear them around my neck for a day.
- He used to spank me, but once I stopped crying out from that, he beat me with the belt. Most times the leather, but

sometimes the buckle. Yes, there was blood, welts, and bruises.

- He would tape the refrigerator and television so he would know if I used them. (I was underweight when the detectives found me.)
- He would hold my hands behind my back so my mother could smack me.
- I was late one day coming home from church, so I couldn't go for a month.
- He didn't want me to go outside and play with the neighbor's kids, because their parents had turned him in for abuse the prior summer, so he called me from his work every half hour to make sure I was home.
- He loved to kick me.
- He started chaining me in the summer of 1956.

I told the interviewer I was just a kid but was expected to be perfect. I was very agitated by the time we were done.

I found out much later they also interviewed my mother and stepfather. Chris Cheek was forty-nine years old, had no children, and had not been married prior to my mother in 1946. He had graduated from Randolph Macon College in Virginia, taught for three years, and then was made the principal of a school in North Carolina for eight years. So why was he now a clerk for a railroad company? That's quite a step down the career path. My guess is that something happened to make him leave that position in education. Could it have something to do with the behavior he was exhibiting with me? I don't know the answer to that, but it certainly sounds plausible. My mother was raised on a farm, had graduated high school, and married at nineteen. She had worked mainly as a waitress.

They didn't deny the punishments but thought they were justified. They stated I was punished for not making my bed, for being late, for not doing my chores, for playing with matches, for lying, etc.

The interviewer said they seemed more upset about the negative reaction of their coworkers to what they had done than the actual deeds themselves. As I said before, my picture with the chain on my leg had been in the paper, and it sounds like they caught some heat for their actions. Chris Cheek asked the interviewer not to tell his family he had been charged with assault on a child. He said he would rather be electrocuted than for them to find out!

They also interviewed the neighbors, my sixth grade teacher, and the priest at Church of the Ascension. All of them said I was a normal boy and showed no problems to them. But I was not normal; 34th Street had taken its toll! On the outside I was fine, but inside I was a mess.

On a different day before my scheduled court appearance, I was also tested by a psychiatrist. This did not go well. As I sat down in his office, he asked me a few questions about my stepfather. I said, "I hate him and wish he were dead." It went downhill from there.

The doctor showed me some pictures—the Rorschach inkblot test—and asked me what I saw for each one. I quickly tired of this and began saying they all looked like bats or butterflies. Out came the blocks, and I was asked to form them into the shape shown on a piece of paper. I couldn't do it. I knocked the blocks off the table, and said, "I'm too old to play with blocks."

We took a short break after that, and I calmed down a bit. At the close of the visit, I told him I didn't like anyone trying to "figure me out"— that what I thought was my business.

Here are some things he stated in his report, which were relayed to the judge:

+ His tests indicated attempts to deal with feelings of hostility and to repress his aggression.
+ Shows a need to manipulate the situation in which he finds himself.

- The tests showed an emotionally disturbed individual with a potentiality for developing a serious mental disease in the future.
- He is enuretic and sucks his thumb when no one is looking.
- His teacher reports he could do much better in class.

All this was a far cry from when we moved to Norfolk in 1949. My sister said I was living with the Pope family in Atlanta, and when I moved to Georgia in 1949, I was a well-adjusted five-year-old, happy with a good personality. Chris Cheek, and, indirectly, my mother, had done a number on me!

Here's the summary of the investigation, interviews, and clinical tests that was given to the judge:

This is a situation of a child whose father deserted the mother prior to the child's birth. After he was born, he was placed in boarding houses and remained there until he was about five and a half years old at which time he was brought into the home of a mother who was a stranger to him plus a new stepfather. Even after this, Michael did not have a feeling of security because since he has been in Norfolk he has been in several boarding homes or left in the care of a colored maid. Michael is rebellious and expresses hostility towards his stepfather and also is appearing to resent the relationship between his mother and Mr. Cheek.

Because of his parents' frequent absences from the home due to their employment, he has been left by himself where, no doubt as a result of boredom, he has gotten into mischief and done things that the family finds irritating. Michael no doubt needs a warm affectionate home where he can find security and satisfaction.

Mr. Cheek, the stepfather, who purportedly has a background of teaching experience, and displays symptoms of being a strict disciplinarian and perfectionist, has expected too much of Michael. He has resorted to unaccepted methods of disciplining the boy which has only increased the hostility and resentment, in his relationship with this child. Mrs. Cheek has condoned her husband's actions and rationalized by saying that she herself could not cope with all the problems so that she welcomed Mr. Cheek's assistance in dealing with Michael.

She says that she has done many material things for Michael such as working hard all of her life to pay his board, however, she does not display any particular warmth when she discusses her son. Mrs. Cheek has on several occasions recognized that there was a problem with her son and has sought help but failed to carry through on suggestions made. It appears at this time that Michael's removal from the home is clearly indicated. Mrs. Cheek and Michael both feel that placement in a boy's school would be beneficial to everyone concerned. I recommend that Michael be placed in the custody of the Social Services Bureau. I do not believe that Mr. Cheek would respond to probation.

Unchained

4

HE IS A VERY GOOD BOY

The phone rang one evening, and after exchanging pleasantries with the person who called, Etta handed the phone to me.

"Michael, its Reverend Rose. How are you?" I was so excited to hear his familiar voice! I told him I was doing well and that I missed singing in the choir and missed the doughnuts in his office!. We didn't talk about what had happened, just shared some small talk. I was loose, smiling, and when I hung up the phone, Etta came over and gave me a big hug. She told me that he had called earlier to check up on me, and that it was obvious to her that he cared for my well-being. As I lay in bed that evening, I thought about the short phone call and how much I liked Reverend Rose.

As I mentioned earlier, my sister, Celia, had begun taking me to church when I was about six. She had spent several years in an Episcopal home for girls in Georgia, and Church of the Ascension was just a few blocks from our home on 34th Street. Church of the Ascension became a haven from the storm for me. I continued going by myself and was excited that I was able to sing in the choir as I got older. At one of the services during the Christmas season I stood in front of the entire congregation and sang a solo! *O Come, O Come, Emmanuel* has continued to be one of my favorite hymns. Reverend Rose often invited me into his office after the service where he always had an extra doughnut or two for me.

I was also particularly fond of one of my Sunday school teachers: Mrs. Virginia Danner. She lived with her daughter's family, and on several occasions, I was invited to eat Sunday supper with them, which was invariably waffles and sausages—with hot melted butter and syrup!

It wasn't until many years later I found out what the angel disguised as a priest had done on my behalf. His exact words as he telegrammed Bob Burrowes, the Director of Boys Home, July 12, 1956, a mere four days after the arrest of my stepfather.

> Dear Mr. Burrowes:
>
> We have a young boy who sings in our choir who is in need of a permanent home. Last weekend, an incident involving the boy created quite a bit of publicity in Norfolk—was in the newspaper, etc. The boy has been mistreated by his mother and stepfather. The latest incident was the stepfather's chaining of the boy. He is a very good boy, 12 years old, much in need of care and affection. I have talked with the Officers of the Juvenile and Domestic Relations Court, and we believe that a place like Boys Home is the best answer to his problem. He has been in foster homes before and has been shipped from 'pillar-to-post' many times.
>
> Is there a possibility of his being admitted to Boys Home? What are the financial arrangements, etc.?
>
> I would greatly appreciate your concern in this matter. Thank you very much.
>
> Very truly yours,
> Frank L. Rose, Jr.
> Rector

Mr. Burrowes quickly replied that Boys Home would be full at the start of the school year but encouraged Reverend Rose to have the necessary paperwork filled out, and have Social Services get the results of a physical and psychological tests ready just in case. As it turned out, there was an opening at the last minute, and the social worker told me I was headed to Boys Home soon!

I had to stop writing for a couple of days after typing the above letter into the manuscript. My heart hurt over six words; "He is a very good boy." I had been told for years, over and over, what a very bad boy I was by my mother and stepfather. And then mistreated emotionally and physically for it. The emotional part was much worse in the long run. It took me many years to soften my heart and heal those emotional scars. Was I deep down a bad person? No, but oh how I wish I had seen that letter Reverend Rose wrote those many years ago.

They pulled me away from my mother just outside the courtroom door after the judge had made his decision. She was hysterical, grabbing at me as the judge had just ruled that she was not to have any contact with me until I left Boys Home, which turned out to be seven years later. I was staying with the Walkers at this point, but still I had strong feelings for my mother. I was torn in how I felt about her. Even though she wasn't a good mother and let Chris Cheek abuse me, she was still my mom. It wasn't until later that I hardened my heart toward her, and slowly but surely put her out of my mind.

Unchained

SECTION TWO
BOYS HOME OF VIRGINIA

Unchained

5

LIFE ON THE HILL

The stated mission of Boys Home of Virginia is basically the same now as it was when I arrived on campus Thursday, September 13, 1956: "to help each student strive toward becoming a productive member of society, by developing his spiritual, mental, physical, and social potential."

In layman's terms, that means turning a boy into a man. They had their work cut out for them with me, that is for sure.

Boys Home was started as a farm school in 1906 by an Episcopal priest and moved up to "The Hill" by the end of World War I. It's called The Hill by everyone because it literally sits on a hill about three quarters of a mile from U.S. Route 60, just three miles from Covington, Virginia. I was used to flat ground, but there were mountains all around when the social worker dropped me off. I remember that I was happy-go-lucky when we left the Walkers and Norfolk, but by the time we hit Covington, I was a nervous wreck! Thankfully I didn't have to attend school the next day, so I had a long weekend to get acclimated to my new surroundings. I was scared—so much to learn and adjust to.

I woke in a panic and realized I had wet the bed again! I really couldn't remember a time over the past three years when I would go more than a few days with dry sheets. It wasn't until much later that I realized there wasn't anything I could do to stop it, and that the cause was anxiety and fear. The guilt, embarrassment, and fear hit home as usual, but this incident was different. I had just come to Boys Home and was sleeping in a dorm room with several other boys. I was so afraid that I would be found out, laughed at, and made fun of. I had learned what to do when I awoke with that wet, warm feeling—usually brought on by a dream that had me peeing. It was a pleasant feeling until I woke up.

I was lucky this time, as it was in the middle of the night, which would give me time to get the sheets dry by morning. I had been through this drill before. I did this by laying on the wet part, letting my body heat dry the sheets. But what if I didn't get them completely dry, I thought? I decided to stay up all night and get up and make my bed just before the other boys woke up.

It didn't go as I had planned, as I kept dozing off and waking up. Luckily it turned out all right, as I awoke just before our housemother, Mrs. Watkins, came in to get us up. I made my bed, grabbed a book, and was sitting on the edge of the bed when Mrs. Watkins walked into the dorm room. The other boys got busy making their beds, putting clothes on, and hitting the bathroom.

Whew, I had not been discovered. This pattern went on for a couple of months, with me frequently wetting the bed, then finding ways to hide it.

We had house chores every day before we went to school, but on Saturday mornings, we gave the cottage a deep clean, and turned in our soiled sheets, washcloths, and towels for clean ones. I was surprised that my sheets never seemed to have yellow stains or pee smell.

At some point, I realized what was happening. Mrs. Watkins would wait until we had gone to school, and then check my bed. If she needed to, she would change my sheets, but not with clean ones. She didn't want me to know she knew my secret. She never said a word about my bed wetting to me, quite unlike my mother or stepfather when I lived with them. Shortly after I realized what my housemother was doing, my bed wetting became more and more infrequent, until it no longer was a part of my life.

Nobody paid me any mind as I walked into the dining hall for supper. Trailing behind my cottage mates. I quickly became acclimated to the ebb and flow of campus life, all dictated by "the bell." I stood by my chair with my cottage mates and housemother and tried to pay attention to what was next. An older boy stepped forward to say grace, and everyone got quiet. After the "Amen," it got really noisy as eighty-plus boys and staff got busy eating.

The food was served family style, with large platters of steaming hot food and all the milk you could drink. Several older boys were assigned to bring out the food and milk and go back for seconds when needed. This chore rotated according to a posted list. I found that often there weren't enough "seconds" for everyone, and this led to guys stuffing their faces quickly and sending the empty platters or bowls back for more. This led to the "grace" before the meal that everyone knew but was never spoken out loud; "Praise the Father, Son, and Holy Ghost, the one that eats the fastest gets the most"!

On Sunday morning after breakfast, I learned we were all going to church in Covington. I was glad I had my new suit to wear. I looked sharp! The bell rang and we headed to the front of the dining hall to board the two yellow school buses with "Boys Home" written in black on the side— mostly the older boys on one bus, and the rest of us on the other. Emanuel Episcopal Church reminded me a lot of Church of the Ascension in shape and size, and of course the service was very familiar, as we used the same prayer book. I noticed there were varying degrees of participation among the boys, and I saw more than one sleepy head jerk sharply upward during the sermon. All the hymns were familiar to me, and by the time the service was over, everyone around me knew I loved to sing.

We got back to the cottage, changed our clothes, and after some hang out time, it was on to lunch. After lunch, I played in my first of many pickup football games on the "field." Most of the buildings on the main campus were situated in an oval around a very large open field. I was walking around minding my own business and stopped to watch the game.

One of the high schoolers yelled over at me, "Hey you, get out here. We need an extra player." That was to be my first introduction to the "pecking order" at Boys Home. I hollered back that I was not interested in playing, and before I knew it, I was being pulled by my ear out onto the field. The big boys ran the show of course, and all the little or younger boys were put on the offensive and defensive lines. Our job was to either rush the passer or block for the passer. It was a while before I actually touched the ball on the Hill. It felt good though to run around and be a part of the group.

6

THE BULLY

The next day was to be my first day of school. As per the routine, I quickly learned it was: wake up, make your bed, hit the bathroom, brush your teeth, etc., then down to the dining hall for breakfast, and back to the cottage. Household chores were next, with everyone being assigned a daily task on a rotating basis. Let me tell you, those cottages were kept immaculate. Of course, as a new boy, my first assignment was cleaning the bathroom, and after some instructions from our housemother, I only had to do it over twice. Then we got our school clothes on and headed down to the bus for school.

Boys Home Boys attended public schools in Covington—with one exception. There was a little three-room schoolhouse just down the hill near the entrance to Boys Home. I couldn't believe I was going here for school. A three-room schoolhouse? With a wood-fired potbellied stove for heat? One classroom was a combined third and fourth grade class, and I was placed in the other classroom which was a combination of fifth and sixth graders. As I've stated earlier, I had already passed the sixth grade, and so I thought it was stupid of them to make me repeat that year in school. Of course, the curriculum was a little bit different from the school in Norfolk, but the math, science, and history were basically the same.

I spent most of my class time studying Shelby Charles. She was very pretty, was physically mature for her age, and she became my first big crush!

My teacher was a nice lady who had her hands full with the Home Boys and the other students. I'm sure it was hard for her to keep everyone on task, and to prepare lessons for two different grades. In order to preserve her sanity, we had several recesses during the day, and if we got our work done correctly, we could be let out much earlier than the other students. I really honed my recess skills as the year went on and got in a lot of extra reading outside of the normal curriculum.

Being outside early kept me away from the bully, Sidney Edwards, who was also in the sixth grade and in my cottage. He wasn't the best at schoolwork, and often missed recess altogether as he wasn't allowed out until he finished his assignments. There was a set reward/discipline system at Boys Home, and you could earn a little extra spending money by making the honor roll. I determined early on that I needed all the money I could get my hands on, so I was typically on the A/B honor roll, and pulled in a little extra money each week. After the first day of school, I thought that this sixth-grade year was going to be a piece of cake.

It was not all smooth sailing, however. Sidney was a classic bully, lording it over anyone he could control. It didn't take him long to target me. Sidney was from Nora, Virginia, a very small coal mining town in southwest Virginia. Wikipedia says this about Nora: "Up through the 1960s, Nora was known locally as 'Tiger Town', because the tiny village had three taverns, resulting in frequent alcohol-induced brawls."

I guess Sidney was just a by-product of his environment, but that was no consolation to me. He was a short, barrel-chested boy, about my age, with what I thought was a thick redneck accent. Like any bully, Sidney's first order of business was to find out if I would fight back when provoked. He found an excuse to smack me a couple of times, and when I didn't strike back, he knew he had another easy mark.

Now you've got to understand, in 1956 there was a very different interpretation of bullying than we are accustomed to today. In many cases, it was expected that a boy was going to get picked on ("bullied" in today's vernacular), and that, as a rite of passage, he had to learn to defend himself. Now if there was a big difference in age and size, some adult would usually step in and make sure the victim didn't get pushed around too much. For the most part, at Boys Home in those days, you had to learn to deal with problems like that as best you could. It wasn't that folks didn't care; it was just part of the growing up process among boys. And besides, usually it was done when no adult was around. The worst thing you could do was to tattle on someone else. A definite no-no, which brought swift reprisals and no sympathy from the other boys.

At Boys Home, just like a lot of other places then and now, a definite pecking order was established. You had to work your way up the ladder. Of course, it wasn't like guys were getting the crap beaten out of them by a bully, they just had to be at his beck and call. It could be subtle or overt, depending on the situation. Sidney wasn't the subtle type, and I'm positive he didn't even know the meaning of the word, much less how to spell it. Usually, he would just make fun of me, or make me fetch something for him, you know, just to make himself feel better.

Saturday was the day we got our allowance, right after lunch. Then the younger boys would get loaded onto the bus and dropped off in town for the afternoon. We would walk the streets, go to the movies, or try to sneak into one of the pool halls around Covington. Around five p.m., the bus would be in a central location; we would pile on the bus and ride the three miles back to The Hill.

I know, you are on the ground laughing about a twenty-five-cent allowance, but the Saturday matinee at The Strand Movie Theatre was only fifteen cents, and I could get a coke and popcorn with the dime I had left over.

As I came out of the dining hall after lunch the next Saturday, Sidney had his hand out and demanded I hand over the twenty-five cents I had just been given for my weekly allowance. I didn't want to give it up, but he said he would kick my butt when we got to town if I didn't give it to him right then.

Sure enough, when the bus drove away after dropping us off in town, Sidney roughed me up until I gave him my quarter. Now I know what some of you are thinking: Why did you put up with that? Good question. In my case, I had just been uprooted from my family (thank God) and I had a lot of uncertainty about what that meant for me. The bullying I got from Sidney was nothing compared to the situation I had left. I was used to being the whipping boy, so it was easy to fall back into that role. And yes, there was fear.

Over time, I learned to keep a sharp eye out for Sidney and to avoid him when I could. It wasn't until later that I learned a most valuable lesson about bullies: They really don't want to fight—they just like the power they have over someone else. If you stand up to them and fight back, even if you lose, after a couple of times, they will leave you alone and turn their attention to someone else.

Things went along for some months, and then, poof, Sidney was gone. I don't know why he left, or what happened to him, but my life immediately was changed for the better.

I did see Shelby Charles one more time after sixth grade while I was in high school. A former Boys Home Boy had settled in the area after graduation and had a farm in Johnsons Creek, a small community Northwest of Covington. One day he came up on The Hill looking for boys to help him put up hay. He would pay for the work, feed us, and bring us back that evening. I volunteered for the job, got hot, sweaty, and itchy from the hay bales, but it was good to do something different.

It just so happened he knew the Charles family, and he took four of us over to their house for a short visit after supper. Shelby was a young woman by then and I spent an hour or so sitting next to her on the couch. It was heaven! I never saw or heard from her again, but she has always been one of those "what ifs" in my life. Not that I would have ever wanted to stay in the area around Covington when I graduated. It was not the place for me.

Unchained

7

DAILY LIFE

Sometime later, Dale tried to step into the void Sidney had left. We were eating dinner and because someone was not at the meal, there was an extra piece of pie. I called "dibs" on it before anyone else, but Dale wanted it. He said he would whip my butt if I ate it. I decided it was now or never; I had to stand up for myself. There was this crazy thing about "goosing," so I stuck my middle finger in the pie, knowing no one would eat it after I did that. It was delicious!

After supper, we went to the big field next to the dining hall, with a large group of boys yelling "fight, fight!" That's when I discovered I had a pretty good left jab. The third time I hit Dale, I bloodied his nose. With all the guys there, he didn't want to quit and lose face, so he made the excuse that he had to go and change his shirt because it was a town night, and he was going to the movies. Everyone knew the real reason, so he got made fun of as he walked away. The crowd dispersed quickly as a staff member came up. He asked what had happened and I said just a little disagreement. For that fight and a number of other reasons, I never got bullied again.

Fall comes early in the Alleghany mountains, and that's when I found out that my hand fit a rake perfectly! We had morning and afternoon chores. In the morning we cleaned the cottage, and in the afternoon, we worked on the campus. I'd get home after school, change from my school clothes to my work clothes, and then, on the bell, head down to the administration building by the dining hall for "rack-up." I'm not sure how rack-up got its name because it should have been called work detail. We had a large campus that constantly needed upkeep and cleaning, and rack-up was the laboratory to help teach us the value of work, how to work, and how to work together.

Some boys had permanent jobs like cleaning the chapel, the gym, the administration building, and keeping the coal fired furnaces going in the colder weather. If you didn't have a permanent job, you would find out each day what you were going to be doing. Rack-up usually lasted about an hour and fifteen minutes.

One of the adult men gave out the assignments and any tools for the job. He would then supervise the main work effort, like raking leaves, but often an older, responsible boy would be doing some supervising, working with a smaller group. So, for that boy, it's work and leadership rolled into one. Boys Home taught me the value of hard work, how to work as a team, and as time went on, how to lead. These are valuable life skills.

After supper, I grabbed one of the softer chairs in the small library area and settled in for the one hour of study hall. Homework was the order of the day then, but with a bunch of young kids, the housemother had her hands full keeping all of us focused and on task. My homework was basically a repeat performance of what I completed in school the previous year, so I was free to pull out a book and read. I found that I loved to read, and often would use any free time enjoying my latest volume. It also afforded me some quiet time as there was normally not a lot of that with a cottage full of energetic young guys. It didn't take long for the daily routine to be just that, routine.

Weekends were a totally different story, since having no school left us with a lot of free time on our hands. On Saturday mornings, we followed the same daily routine, except instead of heading to school, we put our work clothes on and headed down to the dining hall area for extended rack-up. This could last for up to three hours and gave us a chance to get more detailed in our campus work, but sometimes it seemed like there was a lot of "make work" to keep us busy. With a three-hour work window, there was a lot more down time, visits to the bathroom, hiding, and leaning on rakes! And then of course after lunch, it was onto the bus for town time. The bus usually picked us up in town about five, and after supper we were free until bedtime, which for the younger boys was between eight and nine o'clock. That free time could be spent outside playing, or maybe watching that small black and white TV with the rabbit ears in the living room.

Sunday mornings meant church in town, and we usually got a shower before putting on our church clothes. We would pile in a couple of Boys Home buses for the trip to Emanuel Episcopal Church, which was in downtown Covington. It wasn't a large church and would probably have seemed pretty empty without all the Home Boys and staff. The order of service was very familiar to me, of course, but most of the guys weren't paying that much attention. Getting up and down for hymns and praying helped keep everyone awake, but a long sermon found a lot of nodding heads and the staff was kept busy. I sang in the choir with a few other guys for a bit, but it wasn't the same for me as Ascension, and so I dropped out. I still enjoyed singing in the pews, however.

After church it was back to the dining hall for lunch, and then, after changing out of our Sunday clothes, we had the whole afternoon to ourselves. There were lots of opportunities to have fun hiking, heading to Dunlop Creek for swimming or fishing, playing ball in the gym or field, or just simply hanging out. It also left time for plenty of mischief! After supper there was a study hall to get any homework done, then the usual lights out preparation.

Unchained

8

HOOPS AND HOLY WATER

I was blessed with athletic ability, and when I arrived at Boys Home, I found a community that both admired and fostered those abilities. Being good at sports brought recognition and admiration among my "brothers." We had all come to Boys Home from different situations and backgrounds, but one of the things we all shared in common was having a feeling of being tossed aside, of being thought of as "less than" or "the other."

Where can one find a sense of self-worth and accomplishment when it seems all is against you, and you are not considered normal? When you want to stand up and say, "Here I am, look at me. I can accomplish something just like everybody else." Sports was our collective vehicle for recognition and status. At Boys Home the individual was important, but the concept that was more significant was that of team, of 'us' versus 'them.' We needed to band together to survive what we were going through.

As I am looking back and speaking through my "voice" of the past, I am speaking of my pride in my accomplishments in that moment because this gave me my sense of identity. Sports has played a unique role in this country, where an individual or team that is successful is held up by the community at large. Players and coaches are admired, respected, thought of as winners. That is what we yearned for!

My hands were sweating; I was so excited as I jogged onto the gym floor! Basketball season had arrived on The Hill! I loved basketball, and was good at the skills for my age, but I had never played on an organized team. Basketball was king on The Hill, with well over half of the guys on one team or another. There was Varsity, J.V., a Scout team (Boy Scouts), and a team called the Hilltoppers comprised of younger guys. All told, there were over forty boys playing organized hoops. There was a kindly older man named "Pop" Newsome, who was going to be the coach for the younger boys. Pop was great for this age group, as he was knowledgeable but gentle and patient. Pop was also the Scout leader on The Hill, and he led a large contingent of Boy Scouts.

I had a lot to learn, as I had never played on a team, just played some pickup games at school in Norfolk. I was a very competitive kid, and I wanted to win at all costs. From the start of my days on The Hill, I spent as much time in that old gym as I could! I don't remember the Hilltoppers playing any games that winter, as we spent our time learning the fundamentals of dribbling, passing, and shooting. All the boys were brought to the gym to watch the varsity play their home games, and we cheered wildly for our brothers, win, or lose.

We had a deacon and his family on The Hill, John R. Dainty, and he led our worship service on Wednesday evenings after dinner. We had a beautiful little chapel, with just enough room for all ninety or so boys plus staff to squeeze in. It made for some rousing singing though, when one of the hymns was familiar to everyone. John R. had a tough job, as he was also one of the men who helped run the daily campus activities, and he was judged differently than the other staff because he was a "holy" man. I got along well with him and enjoyed sitting with him and his family during meals. He had a very nice, quiet, diminutive wife, and two young daughters.

I think I had talked with him about going to an Episcopal church in Norfolk, and he asked me if I had been baptized. I told him no, and that my mother and stepfather never went to church or showed any interest in what

I was doing there. He said there were going to be a couple of classes soon that would teach about baptism, and asked if I would be interested. I said sure, and before I knew it I was having water poured over my head, and "marked as Christ's own forever."

I thought it was fun and enjoyed it, but I didn't notice any change in me or my behavior. My brothers on The Hill sure didn't treat me any differently! At first, I felt a little guilty if I did something I shouldn't have, like lying or cursing, but that feeling disappeared quickly. Obviously, like many, I'm sure, I was a little too immature at the time to understand the significance of the "sign of the cross" on my forehead. But it was an important step in my ongoing faith journey.

The rest of my first year on The Hill was filled with the daily routine of life. That was one of the secrets of success at Boys Home, learning to do the same thing, over and over, and hopefully doing it the right way. I went about my business flying under the radar. And dreaming about Miss Shelby Charles!

Unchained

9

THE RUNAWAY

During the summer, a few of us were moved into the newly completed Jack Gordon Cottage. We were soon joined at the start of the school year by some new boys on The Hill, so there was a lot of "new" to handle. Unfortunately, I didn't handle it well.

The cottage had a basement with a laundry area, and a large space with a cement floor where we could hang out. On the main floor, were two dorm rooms for the fifteen or so boys, a houseparent suite, living room and small kitchen. The second floor consisted of apartments for staff housing. Mr. Robert "Chief" Burrowes, who became director in 1946, had raised a lot of money, and used it to modernize The Hill and add several new buildings and cottages. Jack Gordon was the latest.

Seventh grade proved to be my worst year on The Hill. I didn't get along well with several of the boys in the cottage, and had a big conflict with our new housemother, "Ma" Reed. I demanded a lot of attention and had my own ideas about how things should be done. The cute little blond boy had become a royal pain in the ass! I spent most of that year with a "bar" hanging over my head.

A bar meant you were barred from all privileges as a result of something you had done, or something you had not done. I had to work an extra hour over and above my normal morning or afternoon duties to erase every bar I accumulated. The thing is, bars were typically handed out in groups of three, which meant three extra hours of work to get back into good standing! So, no allowance or going to town on weekends if you still had a bar. It was a great system of accountability though, whether I liked it or not.

The extra work had to be done when there was free time, and it had to be supervised by the person who handed out the discipline. So, the first thing I learned in that regard was that I needed to apologize for my actions, or somehow there was never any extra work to be done, or the staff member who administered the bar was "too busy" to deal with me. I didn't have to grovel, just name the offense, and apologize.

The adult who gave the bar also had the option to direct you to another staff member for the work, and I quickly learned who to go to if that was the case. Some were easier on me than others! There were many times that school year when I saw town only for school and church. I was never hit, spanked, or had any other physical punishment administered by a staff member during my time on The Hill. What a blessing!

My school situation had changed, and now I was in the seventh grade at Jeter Junior High. We caught the school bus down by the dining hall and the nearly three-mile ride to town was often very interesting, as there were only Home Boys on the bus. Now I did get the paddle a few times at Jeter, and the principal there, "Ace" Thomas, must have been a baseball player in his youth, as he swung with a fast, high arc! It never really hurt much, even though I would act like he was killing me! Usually, three licks and you were done. I liked Ace, and as I became older, it was almost as if we were friends.

Back at the cottage, Jerry and I were planning our escape! I had just had another blow-up with Ma Reed. I just couldn't keep my big mouth shut! I was done! Jerry and I had been talking about this possibility for some time, and we had asked around about the best way to go about it. We made our plan, and that night as I lay in bed, I was thinking about the two times I had run away while living in Norfolk.

The first time I ran away, I was living on 34th Street in Norfolk. I was eleven years old, soon to turn twelve. My life with my mother and stepfather was getting unbearable for me, and I wanted to get away from my stepfather's abuse. My stepfather was off from work one day and we had gotten into an argument, and I said I wanted to leave and that I was going to run away. He basically said to go ahead. We lived about three blocks from City Park, which had plenty of open spaces, ball fields, and even a small zoo. I took off after dinner with no plan, no food, no anything. I just wandered around City Park till it got dark, and then started to wonder if I had made a mistake. It started to get chilly, so I huddled under this bunch of trees, trying to stay warm. I gave up around ten p.m. and walked home. When I walked in the door my mother rushed up to me and was crying and held onto me. We walked together down the hall to the living room where my stepfather simply said, "I knew you'd come back."

At that point, I determined that if I ran away again, I would be better prepared. And I was. A couple of months later, I left with plenty of warm clothes on my back, and a pillowcase full of canned food. Stuff like sardines, Vienna sausages, potted meat, crackers, etc. (in those days, that's what we took when we had a picnic). There was an empty field with trees and high grass a few blocks from our house, and I had decided to make that my "home base." There were also a couple of abandoned cars there that I could sleep in. I stayed there for three days and nights, until my food ran out. There had been a big storm front coming through the area, and it rained quite a bit.

I was determined not to go back home, and so I decided to go see Mrs. Danner. I walked the two or three miles to where she lived with her son. Everyone was surprised to see me, and wondered why I was not in school. I made up this bald-faced lie about how school had been canceled for a couple of days because of the rain, and that my mother had said I could spend a couple of days with them. I'm sure they knew this was not true, but they didn't call me on it. I was invited to stay with them for a couple of days while "school was out," and so I got plenty of chances to expound upon that lie. Mrs. Danner knew something about my home situation, and so I'm sure she knew I had run away, but she never let on. I'm not sure what went on behind the scenes, whether she called my mother or not.

After a couple of days, I was getting a little antsy and told everyone I was going to walk home, but I left there torn. I wanted to see my mother, but I didn't want to live there with my stepfather anymore. I decided I would head back to the open field and hang out there. I could make money for food by picking up empty soda bottles and selling them for two cents a bottle at this local store. As I was walking down the road, my mother and stepfather pulled up behind me in their car. (My mother later told me they had been driving around looking for me every day.) I saw them and kept walking, and my mother got out of the car and ran after me.

My mother was hysterical, crying and begging me to get in the car. I was crying too, wanting—and not wanting—to go home with them. I told her I couldn't take living with the abuse anymore, and she said it would stop, that he had promised he would stop. We talked and hugged and cried together for about half an hour, and I finally got in the backseat of the car with my mom. Christopher Cheek never said a word as he drove us home.

Three weeks later the belt came out again, along with the verbal and emotional abuse.

Jerry and I did our morning chores and when everyone went to catch the school bus, we headed down the hill behind the campus to walk the railroad tracks to Covington. Once in Covington, our plan was to hitchhike East on Route 60. Hitchhike you say? Yep. In those days, lots of people of all ages would be found with their thumb out, it wasn't a big deal at all. No one worried about being abducted, molested, etc.

We never even made it to town! Both of us got cold feet about a mile down the tracks, and we walked back to The Hill. Of course, there were a few bars administered for that little escapade. The last time I ran away I went by myself. I made it to Clifton Forge, about ten miles east of Covington. It was late in the afternoon when our director, Chief Burrowes, pulled up

beside me on the road, rolled down his window, and asked, "You hungry"?
I certainly was and answered, "Yes, sir!"

I got in his station wagon, and we headed back toward Covington. Chief said someone had called in and said they had seen a boy on the road. We stopped and ate and had a great conversation on the way back. Chief was the first person who told me that I had the potential to have a good life, that I was worthwhile, that I was smart, and that I could determine my future. I felt so uplifted, and I promised I wouldn't run away again. He said he knew I wouldn't, because if I did, he would send me to Beaumont, a juvenile correctional facility. I didn't and he didn't! That day marked a turning point in my life at Boys Home.

I also go by the nickname "Chief" now. Members of my staff at St. George's Camp started calling me Chief in the early nineties, and it was carried on by my ball players and students at Park View High School. I could by no means ever think I could fill the shoes left by Bob Burrowes, yet I often think of this great man when I hear my nickname. Although he stood no more than five-foot-six, he was a giant of a man, who helped teach and lead so many of us boys toward adulthood. Bob "Chief" Burrowes—RIP.

Unchained

10

"STUFF" HAPPENED

I joined the Boy Scouts because there was a basketball team associated with the Boys Home troop, which was comprised only of Home Boys. I was thirteen and was looking for any opportunity to be on a hoop team. Basketball was a big deal on The Hill. We had our own full-sized gym, and, counting the Scout team, we had four teams with forty-five to fifty players out of about eighty boys. Almost everyone played basketball at one level or another.

There was a Varsity and Junior Varsity team, and a team for middle-schoolers called the Hilltoppers. I was hoping to make the Hilltoppers squad again and joined the Scouts to get even more opportunities to play. I remember we had a big jamboree in a place called Goshen in the mountains near Covington. Our troop arrived, got our camp area assignment, and proceeded to get our campsite in order.

As a group, we were competitive in everything, and Scouting was no exception. Our guys wanted to be awarded more merit badges, etc. than anyone else, and we excelled at all of the physical challenges, relays, etc., that the adult leaders had planned for us. I was the one slacker—after all, I had joined the troop to play basketball, and I would just as soon start a campfire using matches and kerosene. I played along for a while, but quickly lost interest when I saw guys being sent all over the large jamboree site looking for "paper bag stretchers," "sky hooks," etc. So, I was certainly wary and on guard when the leaders started talking about the exciting evening ahead called the "snipe hunt." I figured that one out pretty quick and made myself scarce when it came time to muster up for any evening of sitting in trees looking for the elusive "snipe." I wasn't born yesterday!

Basketball season came, and I was in my element. Between the Hilltoppers and Scout teams, I probably got twenty games under my belt that season. Although basketball is a team game, you don't need a team around to hone your offensive skills. Just a ball and a hoop. Being alone with that ball and a hoop was so therapeutic for me. I could get lost in my own fantasies of being Bob Cousy, Jerry West, Wilt Chamberlain, Bill Russell, or any other player I knew of and admired. I actually loved being in the gym by myself, shooting and pretending.

There was never any privacy in the cottage, never any time to sort through things, so the gym became my redoubt. I spent many, many hours on that hardwood floor over the next six years, honing my skills, and yes, I never lost a game while by myself.

It was always the announcer's voice in my head: "Three seconds left, down by one, Nunnally goes up for the shot, IT'S GOOD! They win!" Or if I missed the shot: "NUNNALLY'S FOULED, HE GOES TO THE FOUL LINE FOR TWO SHOTS!" And of course, I figured a way to keep shooting foul shots until my team eventually won the game.

Usually only Roger Mays, aka "Cornbread," would be in the gym with me. Cornbread's job was to keep the gym and floor clean, and woe be unto anybody who stepped on the floor with street shoes on! That gym floor was his pride and joy. Sometimes we played together, but often I wanted to be alone, and he understood. The rhythmic sound of that ball hitting the floor while dribbling was so soothing, and the sound of the "swish" when the ball went through the hoop, touching only the strings, was almost orgasmic for me.

In the spring following the basketball season, the Home Scout troop was scheduled to go on a weekend trip to the Boys Home Dam. Boys Home owned the small dam near the main campus. The dam held back Dunlap Creek from full flow, and I guess at one time had run a mill or produced hydroelectric power. Whatever its origin, it was a picturesque setting with some crude cabins nearby that the Scouts used. The guys said it was a fun weekend, so I went along, and we had a pretty good time swimming and fishing—until right near the end of the trip.

We had cleaned up the campsite and the cabins and had our packs on, ready to walk back, when they lined the new guys up and put a blindfold on each of us. They said we were going on some mystery walk for our initiation into the Troop. While I had my blindfold on, some guys cracked raw eggs on my head, and others put baked beans on top of the eggs and rubbed the mess into my hair. That did it for me; the end of my Scouting career!

Once a month at supper we had a "birthday table," and all the boys and staff who had a birthday during that month would leave their assigned table and eat together. At the end of the meal, they would be presented with a "community" birthday cake. All the lights would be cut off, and the cake full of lit candles would be brought out, with the whole dining hall singing Happy Birthday. Of course, at the end of the meal, and after announcements, there would be a rush of boys from around the dining hall huddled around the table trying to get a piece for themselves.

Now the dining hall we used in '57 was pretty old, and while I'm not sure if it was around when Boys Home moved up to The Hill, it was showing signs of wear. If you looked up, you could see white/grayish blobs stuck to the ceiling. Some of the boys found it amusing, when no staff member was looking, to wet a bunch of napkins and throw them at the ceiling to make them stick. Of course, I would never want to get involved in something like that!

As you entered the dining hall there was a row of rectangular tables on each side, with a big aisle down the middle. The kitchen and dish room were in the back. We had assigned seating at that time, usually with our cottage mates. All the tables had a staff member present to keep order, because mealtime was high energy. We ate family style, with the food being brought out by boys who had been assigned the task. This job rotated, as did the dish crew who washed and put away the dishes and cleaned the dining hall after each meal.

Every week there would be a new list posted, and I enjoyed it when my name came up for the dish crew. There was minimal supervision, we just had to get the job done and pass inspection from a staff member. That gave us plenty of opportunity to mix play with our work. If you had the industrial strength rinsing hose, you could keep guys ducking and moving! We would rinse the dishes, put them through the dishwasher, dry them, and put them away. That was for over a hundred people every meal! We also had to periodically mop the dining hall floor, and that gave us a chance to throw some soapy water down the center aisle, get a running start, and see who could slide the furthest without busting his butt. Of course, busting your butt was fun too. You pretty much came out of the dining hall wet, especially after the evening meal.

One of the most important things I learned at Boys Home was the value of work. The campus, our "home," was a big one, seventy acres or so, with at least ten buildings to care for. We all had to help clean our cottage every morning, and we worked after school and on Saturday mornings to keep the grounds and other buildings looking good. I learned that any job done right is honorable and worthwhile, even cleaning those toilets. In fact, as a senior I took the job of rinsing the dishes in the new dining hall after the weekday meals for a dollar a week extra in my pocket! (They had begun to pay a little bit, and I do mean a little bit, for some of the jobs that went above and beyond). I took that job for a time in college also, for the then-minimum wage of $1.25 an hour. Every child, regardless of their family's financial circumstances, should learn the value of a job well done by doing chores on a regular basis.

I remember the winter night in which the birthday table festivities had an additional twist. We all came in and stood at our tables and waited for the blessing. After we sat down, the food came out and, on this particular night, we had hot dogs and sauerkraut as the main offering. Of course, the dogs disappeared fast, but the sauerkraut wasn't the biggest hit with everyone, including me. With a bottle of ketchup handy though, most anything was edible. Near the end of the meal, the lights suddenly went out, and the glowing cake was presented with a rousing rendition of Happy Birthday. Then there was a yell or too, and as the lights came back on, all eyes turned to a table nearby, where one of the housemothers had a significant amount of sauerkraut on her body and head, with bits even hanging off her glasses!

It was quiet in the dining hall for a bit, as everyone was shocked, and no one wanted to get caught laughing. Then a male staff member came quickly forward to make announcements and to dismiss us. Once he said, "You may ask to be excused" the place erupted with sound! The culprits were eventually nabbed and disciplined. It was hard to keep a secret with ninety sets of eyes, ears, and tongues around. The birthday table tradition continued, as I'm sure it does today, but that was the last time the lights were turned out while the cake was being delivered. The housemothers had an almost impossible job, particularly those in charge of a cottage containing fifteen teenage boys, 24/7, for days at a time. There were bound to be times when disagreements arose, but most were loved and respected by the boys.

I made my peace with Ma Reed, kept my nose clean, and finished out the seventh grade with pretty good marks.

School was out for the summer! During my years at Boys Home, I spent vacation times during Christmas, and two to three weeks in the summer, with the Walkers in Norfolk. It was something I always looked forward to, as they always welcomed me as if I were a member of their family. Etta was usually working during the week, and of course Burley was on the road a lot with his eighteen-wheeler. That gave Joyce-Fay and I plenty of time together, and we were still squabbling during the summer before my eighth-grade year. It was just petty stuff, really kind of like typical brother and sister arguments. I was getting a lot of attention, and my presence was disrupting the normal flow of life in their household, so I'm sure that had an effect. Also, I could be a brat.

Tommy was working as a lifeguard at the Y Club on the beach, and we would hang out there some on weekends. He would have been a rising Junior at Norview High School that year. It was fun watching him work out with his buddies for the upcoming football season, and of course checking out all the young ladies in their swimsuits. It seemed like Tommy always had one of two cute girls buzzing around him. There were also the Baptist church services to attend: Two on Sunday and one Wednesday evening. It was easy living, and I blinked and was back at Boys Home ready to start the eighth grade.

11

NO CHEEK-TO-CHEEK

The eighth grade at Jeter Junior High found me finally accepting my life at Boys Home in a more positive way, and all in all, I had a good year. I was smart enough, but was easily distracted and often didn't put forth a good effort in school. Unlike the seventh grade there, we weren't confined to the same class all day with the same teacher. We changed classes during the day, and I began to become familiar with a lot of students I would be in school with for the next five years. My graduating class of '63 was the first class that attended high school grades nine through twelve in Covington. Covington was a mill town, and lots of kids went right to work in a mill after graduating in eleven years of school. There was a postgraduate year that could be taken on a voluntary basis by those students who needed additional classes for acceptance to college.

Rock and roll music had slowly reached Covington, and we had informal dances as part of physical education classes every other Friday for some of that year. I loved music and singing, and tried to keep up with the latest from Elvis, the Everly Brothers, Buddy Holly, etc. I was saddened when Buddy Holly and the others were killed in a plane crash in February 1959—we lost a great one there. I learned to do the jitterbug, but my favorites were the slow dances, even though the teachers demanded "arm's length" dancing. Cheek-to-cheek would have to wait for high school. I still sang all the time, and when people got around to telling me how annoying that could be, I didn't care.

P.E. classes were great and gave me an opportunity to test my skills against other guys beyond just the boys from The Hill. I was a natural athlete, blessed with great eye–hand coordination, but I wasn't particularly fast or naturally strong. I absolutely hated to lose, which would prove to be both a blessing and a curse during my life as a player and a coach. P.E. was not coed at that time, and it could get rough and tumble, which was totally encouraged by the male teachers.

Now, we had the Hilltopper basketball team for basketball at Boys Home, and Jeter had their own junior high team, but for some reason we didn't play each other. I do remember that the Boys Home Varsity basketball team had a home scrimmage against Covington High early during my time on The Hill. It ended with a big fight and a Boys Home Boy knocking down a "townie," so maybe that had something to do with it. There was an annual teacher versus student basketball game that winter at Jeter, which was a big deal around school. I didn't play on the school team, but I was the best player in the eighth grade, so I ended up coaching the school team in that game! I don't remember who won, but I remember that I loved my first coaching experience!

The mountains around The Hill could be very beautiful when it snowed, and it seemed like we got a few good snows each winter. Most of the cottages had sleds, and they got good use on the big hill leading down Route 60 near the Boys Home entrance sign. There was a big open field that had probably served as a pasture at one time, and it had a nice slope to it for sledding. That snow hill was fun, but wasn't too dangerous, just a small, often dry little creek bed area to navigate at the bottom of the run, and all would be well. A few minor scrapes or bruises would be the result for most of the guys.

Now there was a hill behind Sams Cottage, near Jack Gordon where I was living, that was an altogether different story! It was a short, steep, curvy path that led down to an unpaved service road below our main campus. The road was used to access the railroad tracks that ran behind the campus, East toward Covington, and West toward West Virginia. There was a small spur off the main line, with a trestle that served as a bridge for the coal car that would periodically be dropped off full of coal to help heat the buildings on campus. There were coal-fired furnaces in the basement of several of the cottages and other buildings, and a boy was assigned to each to keep the furnace full and fired up during the colder months. It was a dirty job, with coal soot getting on your clothes, in your hair, under your fingernails, etc. As I got older, one of my best friends and fellow athlete Pete Davis, had that task and he ended up with the nickname "Greasy." The coal car was dropped off a few times during the winter, and a staff member would supervise some older boys who would empty the coal from the bottom of the coal car into the Home dump truck, and then unload it to the several furnaces. It was a dirty, potentially dangerous job that required missing a day of school, and after my first time as assigned, I bowed out of that task in the future.

Now, back to the sledding hill. It wasn't that hard to walk, but it was steep and curvy and lined with trees and it took a combination of skill and luck to navigate it on a sled. The real challenge took place at night though, usually just as it was getting dark. I had gotten pretty good on the hill that winter and had learned to tape a handheld flashlight to the front of the sled just so. It was a blast until I hit a tree, which happened almost every trip down. Of course, the victor of the night was the boy who could make it the furthest down before crashing. Everybody crashed, and if you didn't get hurt, that was fun too.

Boys Home was like a prison in that no one ever talked about how they got there. I don't ever remember a conversation with anyone that started with, "Hey, why are you here?" In a situation like we were in, everyone has a story and they don't want to hear yours. Of course, some of us found out something about the past of others who were close friends, but it was usually limited to if they had any siblings (good looking sisters especially— pics?), or where they were from, etc. Nothing really deep. Most of us kept our past to ourselves, and just dealt with each other on a day-to-day basis. It was repression for me, which is not healthy for the psyche. Over time, I built that wall brick-by-brick, until I came to rely only upon myself, and never really let anyone "in" my complete world.

I figured out how to construct an alternative "Nunnally" who learned how to get by and fit in without being vulnerable from an emotional standpoint. That lasted until I left the Home, then all hell broke loose. It took a long, long time for me to knock that wall down and I can still erect it at a moment's notice, which sometimes scares me still.

We used to joke and call ourselves orphans, but I'm sure that was not the case for many. Looking back on it though, we were orphans in a way. Orphans from a normal life. At times I would be jealous and resentful of the townies who left school at the end of the day and went to the comfort and love of their family. But I would never admit that to anyone. In the world I lived in, you kept those kinds of thoughts to yourself.

As time went on however, I, like a lot of the boys, developed a pride in my life on The Hill. We would argue, cuss, and fight with each other all day long, but woe be unto anyone else who messes with one of our brothers. Covington was a small town, and on the rare occasion one of us was having a bit of trouble with a townie, word would spread, and he could count on some quick backup. By and large, we were accepted by our peers in school, and I don't remember any overt prejudice against Boys Home Boys among my classmates.

Of course, this didn't hold true for all of the adults, especially the mothers and fathers who had daughters! Like a lot of minority groups, we were "them" to a certain segment of the population; as in, "I don't want you dating one of 'them'." And after all these years, I want to speak for all of my brothers and thank those parents who said that. All a high school girl who likes a certain boy need is to be told *not* to date him, and that will ensure she does. Young girls are often attracted to the rebels, and we were certainly perceived as that. Of course, we took a certain pride in that moniker.

Unchained

12

BLAST FROM THE PAST

Eight grade was drawing to a close and I got a letter from my sister, Celia! I had been at Boys Home almost three years at that point, and this was the first time I had heard from her. There was a sinister reason for this, as my mother had been continually lying to her to conceal what had happened in Norfolk and thus to conceal my whereabouts. Every time Ceal would call her, and during the course of the conservation ask for me, Johnnie Cheek would lie and make up some excuse as to why I couldn't come to the phone. "Mike's outside playing," or "He's doing his homework," etc. When Ceal had gotten married a year or so after I got on The Hill, my mother lied and made up some excuse as to why I couldn't attend the wedding.

Ceal didn't tell me this when she contacted me, I found this out much later. Ceal eventually found out what had happened to me from my Aunt Beja, and she wasted no time in writing to Bob Burrowes. After a few back-and-forth letters with him and social services in Norfolk, it was arranged that I could visit for a couple of weeks when school was out for the summer. She still didn't know what happened to me, but figured something was up when the welfare folks in Irvington, New Jersey, came to her house to check out the living situation there.

I hadn't seen her in several years by that point, so it took a while to get used to each other, but my sister was such a good and loving person that I fell in love with her all over again! Her husband, Herb, was a great guy also, but he was gone most of the time I was there with his job at a nearby General Motors assembly plant, where he worked in management. They had a young son, Todd, who was talking a little, and he was always saying "Uncle Mike, make-a-believe." So, we "made believe" a lot and became good friends. Herb welcomed me right away into his family and he found out I loved to play sports.

He was a tennis player himself, and belonged to a local tennis club, sporting the white tennis outfit, etc. Somehow, I got hold of a used racquet, and Herb took me to the playground by their apartment and showed me how to grip and swing the racquet properly. Luckily there was a "tennis wall" available where I could hit the ball and it would rebound to me. There was a line drawn on the wall to simulate a tennis net, so I could play imaginary games against myself. The "court" was macadam, and by the end of my two weeks stay, I had worn out several tennis balls and a pair of tennis shoes! I would go to the playground after breakfast, come in for lunch, then right back to the pretend court until dinner. Herb had showed me how to serve and hit all the ground strokes, and he and Celia were amazed at how well I was progressing.

One weekend, Herb took me to his tennis club, and I played on a real court for the first time. Herb was patient with me and didn't try to beat me too bad, and the next Saturday found us out there again. There were a couple of high school boys who were on the tennis team playing against each other, and Herb suggested I play them. They looked young, and probably were ninth or tenth graders, but I beat them both. I was tenacious in chasing any shot they tried to get past me, and my serve was so fast that when I got it inside the box, they couldn't return it. It was a great visit, and I continued my relationship with Ceal, Herb, and Todd from that time on. I read that leatherbound copy of "The Swiss Family

Robinson" that Celia gifted me over and over, and really regretted the day I looked for it and it was gone.

Unchained

13

ONWARD COUGARS

Summer was over. It was September 1959, and time for high school—Covington High School, home of the Cougars. As I stated before, the class of '63 would be the first graduating class that had to attend four years to earn a diploma.

I was grinning from ear to ear when I got on that bus to head to Covington High my first day of ninth grade! In their infinite wisdom, the powers that be had decided that only the Home Boys would be on the bus to and from school. Good decision. There was usually a separate bus for the junior high boys (Jeter Junior High) and those who went to the high school. The big boys who smoked usually sat in the back of the bus, and the guys who wanted that last puff before school would head for the last two or three rows on either side in the back. When we hit the main highway to town, old Route 60, the windows would come partially down, and the cigarettes and matches and lighters would come out. You had to put your head and the hand that held the cigarette just so to enable you to take a drag and exhale without smoke filling up the bus. There was a lot of switching of seats back there to allow for everyone who wanted a puff or two to get satisfied before the bus got into town.

I was a fresh ninth grader, and hadn't earned my spurs in Greene Cottage yet, so I wasn't allowed to be part of the bus smoking crowd. Since we slowed down when we got into town, it would be obvious to anyone watching the bus that there was smoking going on, so the rule was all smokes had to be put out before we hit the stoplight by the Esso station just as we got into town. Of course, the bus driver knew we smoked on the bus, but he never mentioned it or said it was okay. It was understood that if we kept any bad behavior to a minimum, he would look the other way on smoking, etc. I think I remember that we had the same bus driver the whole time I was in high school, but I can't remember his name. Of course, the mutual cease fire didn't last forever, and there were times when he would have to yell at us for one thing or another.

We had a couple of yearly peace offerings for the bus driver though. Every year around Thanksgiving and Christmas there would be a canned food drive at the school for those families in the community in need. We would each be given a couple of cans to take in to do our part. Some boys found that ironic: "Hell, aren't we needy?" they joked. While I was on The Hill, that food never made it off the bus. I'm not sure when the tradition started, but as we departed the bus on those days when we were given canned food, each boy placed his cans on the seat behind the bus driver for him to take home to his family. He would invariably get emotional and choked up and would turn his head away from us while saying, "Thank you boys" as we got off the bus. It made us feel good to help him out, and yes, to earn some brownie points for the future!

It was a little intimidating at first—a new schedule and not knowing where all the classrooms were, but it didn't take me long to start singing in the halls.

There was one small problem though. I had flunked grade eight science. I just couldn't concentrate on the schoolwork. I had what I thought was the most beautiful woman I had ever seen in my life for a teacher. I'll just call her Ms. Johnson. She was tall, thin, and had gorgeous long blonde hair. Ms. Johnson was from Tennessee, and she had that beautiful slow Southern drawl. It would be "niiiight," "riiiight," "Miiiike,"—well, you get the picture. I just couldn't seem to concentrate at all on my work in her class. I was flunking big time. About three-quarters through the year though, I just gave up.

I found out something that made me feel bad about my lack of effort though. It seems that my eighth-grade credits would count toward graduation. The eleven-year system meant that the courses I took in eighth grade would count toward my diploma, so since I had flunked science, I would have to repeat the course. Sure enough, the first day of ninth grade, my counselor told me I had to repeat that class. Naturally I was upset, but what could I do? I argued that since I was in the first four-year graduating class, eighth grade classes shouldn't count. Then I decided that another year of being in Ms. Johnson's class wouldn't be so bad, and this time I would make sure to pass.

They gave me a study hall for fifth period, which gave me plenty of time to walk the half mile back to Jeter Junior High for science class at the end of the school day. There was a big temptation along the way, however: Cunningham's Pool Hall. I loved to play pool, and there was usually just enough time to play a game or two and still make the bell for science class if I ran part of the way. There were three pool halls in the rather small downtown area of Covington in '59, and Cunningham's was the classiest. They had more tables, better tables, better lighting, etc.

Now you don't see a lot of pool halls today, and when you do, they are often not like the ones I ventured into as a youth. Today's pool halls are billiard parlors and are often coed. Clean, sterile environments that remind me of a hospital room. Cunningham's and the other pool halls all smelled the same; smoky, musty, with the faint smell of chewing tobacco spit on the floor around the spittoons. There was always a bit of beef jerky to be purchased, and those huge jars of pickled eggs with the vinegary smell. The clientele was all male, with a great variety of characters. A young boy of fifteen could learn a lot if he kept his eyes and ears open, as the conversations included topics that were not normally discussed in polite or mixed company, if you get my drift. Of course, when some of the old salts could see that I was paying too much attention, then they would have a little fun at my expense. Lots of big yarns would be fabricated, kind of like Paul Bunyan, except the "Blue" in the story didn't have anything to do with an ox.

The conversation would soon enough turn to "When I was your age," and end with some admonition about how to deal with the mysteries of the opposite sex. Luckily, I never got in the position to try out some of that advice. Of course, I was late a few times, and skipped a couple of my science classes because of my stops in Cunningham's. I would get involved in a game and lose all track of time. I had to visit the principal, Ace Thomas, on more than one occasion for a few warm gentle reminders on my backside that I had to be in class on time.

I'm happy to report that I passed the class, and that my backside was none the worse for wear. I walked into that class the first day only to find that Ms. Johnson had moved and was no longer teaching at Jeter. Bummer! Instead, I had a strict, middle-aged man who allowed no nonsense. It was probably for the best, and I ended up getting a pretty good grade.

My new schedule found me taking P.E. first period. Ugh! I was usually up for sports and athletics—but first thing in the morning? I would spend the time in the cottage after breakfast and morning duties getting ready for school, and the sweat and messed up hair after class was not a good look. I, like so many of the high school boys, took pride in how I looked. I had to look good for the ladies! Not that I had any chance, but hope springs eternal.

There was one day in the fall, however, when something happened that made me so glad I had that early P.E. class. After every home football game, it fell to the first period boys' P.E. class on Monday to clean up all the trash that had been thrown under the bleachers during the game Friday night. This was not how any of us wanted to start our school week, and it took a lot of cajoling and threats from our teacher to keep us on task. Every now and then someone might find something of interest down there, but it was messy work that required a lot of bending over.

One day I hit the jackpot on the visitor's side of the bleachers. There was usually not a big crowd of folks following their team to Covington, as it was situated in the Alleghany Mountains a long drive of an hour or more from most of the other high schools in the Blue Ridge District. Consequently, there was not as much trash to pick up on the visitor's side, so I headed for that side of the field whenever I could, just shuffling around under the bleachers trying to look busy. After the third home game I was doing just that, and as I looked down, there it was! A picture of Andrew Jackson staring up at me, with the number twenty on either side of the top of the bill!

I wasn't sure at first what it was, then I remembered I had seen Burley Walker pull a roll of those out of his pocket to pay for our dinner at a truck roadhouse. Twenty bucks. I was rich. I bent down, picked it up in a wad, looked around quickly, and shoved that thing as deep in my pocket as I could. As much as I liked to talk and brag, I told no one about that gift from heaven for a long time. I kept it buried deep in my footlocker in Greene cottage, and every once in a while, when I was sure no one was around, I would sneak it out for a quick peek.

"Welcome to bonehead math." That's what I heard on the first day of ninth grade from my math teacher. Now I wasn't the brightest bulb at CHS but I thought, "I'm a damn sight brighter than bonehead math!" So, during study hall period that day, I signed up to see the counselor about changing out of that class. I got called down to her office a couple of days later, and had my first interaction with Helen Thomas, the one guidance counselor in a high school of nearly five hundred students. I explained that I wanted out of bonehead math and asked what my options were. She pulled out my records from Jeter, and after looking over them and some of my math test scores, she suggested that I continue with the course I was slated to take. This was to be one of the first times I stood up and advocated for myself, as

I told her I was adamant about changing to a higher math course. Then I asked her what that was, as I really didn't really know! She laughed and told me she would try and get me into Algebra 1. She would contact me in a couple of days.

I didn't realize until later how difficult it was to change a student's class schedule in a small school like CHS. There were only so many offerings of Algebra 1, and none of those was offered during third period, when I was scheduled for ninth grade (bonehead) math. Add to that, the fact that due to my own failure to pass science the previous year, fifth and sixth period were not an option for me to take Algebra 1. Ms. Thomas called me down a couple of days later and showed me my new class schedule, in which every one of my classes had to be changed. I didn't appreciate all the work that took on her part until I became a teacher some twelve years later.

As it turns out, I wasn't quite the math whiz I thought I was, and got by in Algebra 1, but that was it for my Algebra career. It's funny though, I have excelled at bonehead math all my life and learned that it's what you need in the day-to-day of living!

14

CHANGES

Ninth grade changed everything for me, with big changes coming both on The Hill and in school. I was moving into one of the big boys' cottages! I got lucky and was moved to Greene Cottage, which was the top dog at the time. Boys Home was a very competitive environment, and with all the testosterone flowing up there, you either learned to compete or got run over. As I have said before, there was a definite pecking order—defined by both toughness and athletic prowess. This held true in the cottages and on the campus. Nobody had a number, nor was there a list ever published, but most boys knew where they stood. If you didn't know where you stood and crossed over the line, you found out quick! In Greene, I quickly learned to keep my mouth shut and lay low most of the time. I was not a "tough guy" and never became one. In fact, some of the fans of the opposing teams we played later in hoops used to call me "pretty boy," so I wasn't scaring anybody, that's for sure. In Greene Cottage, we wanted to be the best in everything, especially sports.

The living quarters were tight. As I walked in the front door, I saw the stairs to my left and a hallway straight ahead. The houseparents' apartments to the right took up half of the cottage's ground floor. To the left was the living room and a small library. Down the hall to the right of the stairs was a very small, seldom-used kitchen. A walk up the stairs led to one dorm room on the right and one on the left. A couple of steps down the hall was the bathroom—three sinks and a couple of urinals, stalls, and showers. Obviously, it got really crowded in there at times, especially when that morning wake-up bell rang! Further down the narrow hall was a very small nine-by-fifteen room on the right, where the two proctors lived. The proctors were two older boys who helped the housemother keep order. One of the dorm rooms held six boys, the other room had seven beds. There were two built-in drawers for each boy to keep his clothes in, and above those, some room to hang clothes. We weren't allowed to come in the front door but had to come around to the back of the cottage to enter. There was a small, covered porch where we took off our shoes, opened the door facing the kitchen, and turned right to head down the steps to the basement. To the right was where we spent a very large portion of time when in the cottage. The walls were lined with open benches where we sat, and places to put our shoes underneath. The basement is where everything got sorted out, sort of!

Pete Dimick, whose nickname was Redeye, was a character, and immediately made his presence known when he came to live on The Hill. Like me he was a freshman, assigned to Greene Cottage, and he astounded everyone by going out for the Varsity football team. He made it! There were a lot of very good athletes in the history of Boys Home, but no one could remember a ninth grader being on the Varsity football team at CHS. During his next four years on The Hill he became the stuff of legend. He didn't get much playing time on the field that year, but that was to change as he got older. He was the butt of a few jokes on the football team that season, and was involved in one incident everyone heard about— and laughed about. You have to keep yourself clean and dry as an athlete to prevent that nasty, itchy, oozing, rash fungal infection, better known as jock itch. It often shows up down around the groin area in athletes who don't practice good hygiene "down there." It's easy to get and tough to get rid of.

So Dimick got a bad case, and it lingered. It can be painful and, after a couple of weeks, Pete was ready to try anything.

There were a couple of brothers on The Hill named Bobbie and John Dunn. They both played football and were rough and gruff. I pretty much stayed away from them and those "old salts" like them. One swipe from either of them could pretty much break me in half. Dimick was hurting, and one of the brothers suggested he use 'Mr. Clean' on the rash. Mr. Clean was a multi-surface cleaner we used to clean the cottage, bathrooms, floors, etc. It has alcohol in it, as Dimick soon found out. The howling and screaming could be heard all over the cottage just after the first application. Eventually the jock itch was cured, but the laughter and lore over the incident lived on.

The only times during the day when all the boys on The Hill were together were mealtimes, The mealtime bell would ring, and we would meander down and wait outside the dining hall until we were called in. It was always a guessing game on what was going to be served for dinner. I never ate steak at Boys Home but there was plenty of "mystery meat," you know, with the type of gravy on top determining what the dish was called. Actually, I had no complaints about the food, as there was usually plenty of everything, and all the milk you could drink. I've always joked that most everything we ate was a shade of white: milk, rice, oatmeal, cream of wheat, potatoes, white bread, biscuits, gravy, etc. The boys used to joke that the chipped beef and gravy we had over toast was a little short on the chipped beef. It was rumored that they just took the frozen bag of chipped beef and waved it over the big pots of gravy, then put it back in the freezer.

Believe me, I ate heartily of what was served, because we didn't eat again until the next meal. We ate in a central dining hall, and there were no between meal snacks available.

I do want to relate two "steak" experiences I had early in life, both of which remain etched in my memory. For the first one, I will have to backtrack a bit to a time before I became a "ward of the State of Virginia," and landed at Boys Home. I was either eleven or twelve, I can't exactly remember which, and was living with my mother and stepfather in Norfolk. My sister and brother, who are thirteen and ten years older than me, had been out of our house on 34th Street for a few years. It was quite a while before they learned what had transpired in that place after they left. It was one of my jobs to walk and feed our two dogs, Blackfoot, a mutt, and Hippodrome (Hippy), a Scottish Deerhound, but one day I forgot to feed them. I got the belt that night when Christopher Cheek came home from work.

The next day was Sunday, the only day of the week when we could all eat dinner together. We had gone out for our normal Sunday drive, and as usual we took the dogs to run among the sand dunes near Fort Story, a military base near Virginia Beach. All seemed well, and my stepfather announced we were going to have a special treat for dinner, steak! We sat down to the table after my mother finished cooking, and suddenly my stepfather's mood changed. He gave me a look somewhere between a smile and a smirk as he took my steak, cut it in half, and gave one half of it to each of the dogs. He then went to the fridge and pulled out a half-empty can of Kennel Ration dog food. He spooned this onto my plate and said that because I had forgotten to feed the dogs, we were switching meals tonight. It took a while, but I managed to eat it all without throwing up.

Now let's fast forward a few years to the winter of 1960. I had just gotten off the Greyhound Bus in Norfolk, basically, an all-day trip from Covington. It was Christmas vacation time, and almost all the Boys Home Boys were to spend the holidays with families, foster parents, etc. It was a much-needed break for the boys, and I'm sure for the staff as well. Etta picked me up at the bus station, accompanied by Joyce Fay. On the way home, she explained that Tommy, who was a football player at VPI (now VA Tech), would be home that evening as well. The other member of the family, Burley, was on the road with his eighteen-wheeler, and she didn't know exactly when he was coming in.

We stopped at Farm Fresh Supermarket, where Etta was now working as a checker. Wow. It was huge, the first big grocery store I had ever seen. We bought a few things for supper, and as we shopped it seemed everyone knew and liked Etta. I liked her a lot also, as she always welcomed me as a family member whenever I visited. (As this story unfolds, understand that it is not about Etta, she was great; but the story is about the kind of man Aaron Burley Walker was)

We started home, dropped Joyce Fay at a friend's house, and shortly after we got home, Etta asked me if I was hungry, and said she would fix me a hamburger. Soon after the hamburger and a couple of sides arrived for me, Tommy walked in the door. He had stopped to see his girlfriend, Freddie-Sue, on his way home from Blacksburg.

Tommy was the apple of Etta's eye, as well he should have been. Good looking, excellent student, All-State athlete, fine Christian young man, with a very good-looking girlfriend, whom he later married. (Tommy became a career military officer after his time in the Corps of Cadets at VPI.) After greetings and hugs, Etta said she had one steak left in the fridge and she would fix it for Tommy. We were all talking and catching up as Etta was cooking when who walks in the door? Burley. He had just gotten back from Florida, and he had hauled a truckload of bananas to a wholesale warehouse. It was easy to see that Burley was bone tired, but he sat down to talk with us anyway. He lit up a cigarette and asked for a cup of coffee.

Up to that point in time, I had never really spent a whole lot of time with Mr. Walker, (what I called him then) as he was on the road most of the time when I was in Norfolk for holidays. Although he was a rough around the edge's kind of guy, who liked a drink or two out of the house, he always treated me so gently and kindly, as if he understood that I was damaged goods. As we were talking, he noticed that I was eating hamburger and Tommy was eating a steak. He asked Etta about it, and she said she had been saving the steak for when Tommy came home. Without a word of explanation, Burley got up and said that I should follow him.

He said nothing else to anyone, and we went outside and got into the cab of his eighteen-wheeler, which was minus the big trailer. I could see that he was upset, but I wasn't about to ask him why. We went a couple of miles down the road and pulled into a kind of roadhouse for truckers. We went inside and sat down, and when the waitress came over, Burley ordered a whiskey for himself, and told her to bring me the biggest steak they had in the place! Burley and I developed a special bond from that night on. He's passed on now. I love you Burley!

As my first week in high school went along, I became familiar with my schedule, where all the classes were located, and I felt good about the way my life was going. Friday night came, which meant I was going to be able to go to town in the evening for the first time. Once I hit the ninth grade, I could go to town both Friday and Saturday nights if I wasn't barred. This was going to be my first time, so I hooked up with a couple of other younger guys before dinner and we made a plan. As was common then, all the boys ninth grade and up got to town by hitchhiking. After the dismissal we started running down toward the main road, Route 60. Some other guys were running also, trying to beat us down there. Why were we running? To try and get across the road and stick our thumbs out and get a ride before the big boys got down the hill. It wasn't usually that hard to get a ride, as the local folks knew it was the Home Boys when they saw us on the road. The ever-present pecking order was in play. The top dogs walked down the hill at their leisure and ran the little mutts back across the road to wait in line. Only three boys at a time were typically waiting for a car to stop and pick them up. If there was more room in a car that stopped and the driver indicated it was alright, then another boy or two might be allowed to hop in. With thirty-plus high school guys trying to get to town, sometimes it took a while for everyone to get a ride. Of course, a guy could always try to rearrange the pecking order, but that meant a fistfight. Usually, everyone knew their place, and there weren't that many fisticuffs.

When our little group finally got to town, we walked to the closest local movie theatre, the Strand, with just enough time before the main feature. I had enough left over from my allowance for popcorn and a soda. We had to be back by ten p.m., so we walked around a bit, then headed back to the Esso station to put our thumbs out and get a ride home. It was easier to hitchhike home because guys usually trickled back instead of coming all at once. To get back to the administration building to check in by ten could be tricky though. Most of the time, it was fine to be dropped off at the entrance on the way back, then walk on up to The Hill to check in. When time was running short though, a guy who was a smooth talker could convince the driver to drive all the way up to drop guys off. This is one of the ways in which I honed my smooth-talking skills. Who could resist the cute blond kid when he gave them the sob story about getting in trouble for being late!

CHS, home of the Cougars, was a small high school, so it didn't take long for ninth graders to get acclimated, and the upper-class students tried to have some lame "initiation" for us freshmen, trying to copy what a lot of colleges did in those days. It was harmless, and I for one didn't take it seriously. One time I was sent outside to count the number of bricks in a certain section of the wall. I hung out there for a few minutes, came back and told the guy some absurd number. He said that couldn't be right, and I said, "Then go out there and count them yourself." The good thing about the initiation period was that when it was over, there was a dance honoring the ninth graders. And yours truly got to sing a song for a slow dance! *Dream*, by the Everly Brothers, who had a lot of hits in those days. The dance and that song gave me a bigger profile around school for the rest of the year. Despite that, I still hadn't gotten my first kiss!

Fall of '59 was beautiful in the Alleghany mountains, and as the trees were losing most of their leaves, it was my favorite time of year—hoops time! I had been in the gym working hard. I was about five-foot-ten, but skinny as a rail. I used to tell people that I was so skinny that if I turned sideways and stuck out my tongue, I'd look like a zipper. I couldn't jump that high, and wasn't fast, but I had a knack for getting the ball in the basket. To me there is no better sound than that swish—that "string music"—as the ball goes through the net without touching the backboard or the rim. I made the JV team with a couple of the guys I would be soon playing with on the Varsity: Redeye and Pete Davis.

The Hilltopper Varsity had a good team that winter, but the young guns were looking to the future. We knew that next year we would have a tradition to uphold, but more importantly, we hated to lose, and could be competitive to the point of being nasty. That's what we had learned was a distinguishing feature of being a Boys Home Boy. I don't remember our record, but I do remember we had a rough time getting back into the flow after we came back from Christmas vacation. Almost two weeks off from games and practice had a big effect, especially with young guys. I never touched a ball during that break, didn't run at all to stay in shape, and really wasn't thinking about hoops at all. It was the same for my teammates, and we learned a valuable lesson that we took into the future.

Springtime came and I tried out for the baseball team. There was no JV team, so it was Varsity or nothing. I had a good arm for my age and made the team. Most of that season found me on the bench during games and throwing a lot of batting practice. The older guys basically paid me no mind, as I was a freshman and didn't really contribute. When I wasn't pitching batting practice, I was sent to the outfield to shag balls hit in batting practice. I was in the outfield one day minding my own business when Mickey Caviness asked me if I wanted some chewing tobacco. Lots of boys smoked and chewed, and I didn't want to be thought of as a wimp, so I stuck out my hand and he put a chunk of the chew into my palm. No instructions, no warnings. Within ten minutes I was on the ground, dizzy, sweating, and throwing up. I didn't know you weren't supposed to swallow the juice! In addition, it was plug tobacco called "Days Work," the strongest you could chew. That marked the end of my chewing tobacco days. For some reason, I got a varsity letter for baseball, but I knew that every dog has his day, and my day would come soon enough.

Once school was out for the summer, we went into summer schedule mode until we all headed home for a summer break. The daily schedule obviously changed, with more time for rack-up, free time during the day for play outside, and more free time in the cottage in the evenings since there was no study hall. Most of our free time in the cottage was spent in the basement for one simple reason: that was the only place smoking was allowed on campus, Yes, smoking was tolerated once a boy moved into one of the big boy cottages! The legal age for smoking and buying cigarettes was sixteen, and there was no way for the houseparent, almost always an elderly woman, to monitor who was smoking down in the basement and who was not.

Smoking was thought to be cool, and commercials on TV glamourized its use. There had been some preliminary research pointed toward the serious effects of smoking, yet it was still accepted behavior in the population as a whole. In 1960, forty-two percent of Americans smoked, and that percentage was even higher if you counted kids under sixteen. For a Home Boy who had the money, it was easy to get his older cottage mate to buy "cigs" for him.

There was a whole subculture based around cigarettes on The Hill, and that spilled over into when we were at school or in town on weekends. If boys saw a guy lighting up and they had no smokes, the first guy who hollered "I got your butt" wasn't really trying to grab some hind parts, that meant you had to save the butt, or last bit of the smoke, for him. Of course, that might lead to an argument over who called for the butt first, or blaming the smoker because he didn't save you enough at the end. Like in prison, smokes were money on The Hill. So, I might loan a cigarette to Dimick or my good friend, Richard Nuckols, but everybody else must pay or take out a loan. Typically, the going price was two cigs for a nickel. That was a good profit, as a pack holding twenty smokes was fifteen cents. Of course, there were some guys who always had cigs for sale, that's how they supplemented their allowance. They might sell one for five cents. I started smoking early on and continued off and on throughout my whole life.

A lot of gambling also took place down in the basement, and on The Hill in general. I was pretty good at poker, when we played five-card stud and seven-card stud. We also played other games. A game I never see these days we called "pitch to the line." The players each take a turn tossing a coin of the same value to see who could get closest to a designated line on the floor without going over the line. We had to pitch from behind another line about ten feet away. Closest to the line without going over the line took all the money. Another similar game was pitching the coins toward the wall, and whoever ended up closest to the wall, whether you hit it or not, took all the coins. Lots of opportunity for disagreements!

Another gambling game we called "matching." It went this way. Let's say Redeye (one of Pete Dimick's nicknames; he had red hair) and I were playing the "match." Each player would flip the same value coin, let's say a nickel, into the air, catch it in one palm, and as he turned his palm over, he placed it on the top of the opposite hand. If they both show either heads or tails, they are "even." If they don't match, they are "odd." Each player takes turns calling "odd" or "even" before the tosses are made. Winner takes the coins. Basically, this is a game of luck, as heads or tails will come up randomly. I never made a lot of money with that game.

Of course, Redeye and I never gambled against each other, unless it was cards with a group of guys. We didn't want to take each other's money. We did gamble as a team however, and it's one of the things I regret doing as a youngster, because we were cheating. This game was called "odd man," and involved the same flipping of coins as "match," but this was played with three guys. The winner was the boy whose coin showed different than his opponents. For example, I had a "head" and Redeye and the other guy had "tails." I won. Here's where the cheating came in. If you take a coin, say a dime, and rub your thumb across it with force, you can determine if it's a head or a tail. That knowledge allows you to "feel" the head or tail as you are putting it on the back of your hand and change the outcome as you are placing it. So, a simple "you hold a head and I'll hold a tail" makes sure the game comes up odd, and either Redeye or I will win. We would pocket the winnings and divide it up later. We also devised a system whereby we would lose to the other guy occasionally, so he didn't catch on to the scam. It was wrong, sure, and it really didn't amount to much money, but for me it was about the competition and winning. Sorry guys, I owe you!

The basement was also where disagreements were worked out. Weightlifting, ping pong, and "knee tackle" football, and talking smack were also on the agenda. "Knee tackle"? Yes, even with cement floors and cinderblock walls we would wrap T-shirts around our knees and "run" without standing up. Always a few bumps and bruises during those games. It got loud and rowdy in the basement at times, but the housemother seldom came down the steps, preferring to let us have our space.

I spent time that summer with the Walkers in Norfolk, getting a lot of swimming and girl-watching in at the beach! I also hung out with my sister's family in New Jersey for a few days. Before I knew it, my sophomore year was on the horizon.

Unchained

15

TAKING STOCK

I had been at Boys Home for nearly four years and was just cruising along. I was doing well in school, nothing special, but enjoyed my fellow classmates. On The Hill I got along well with the staff and my fellow brothers, but of course there were times when things weren't going the way I wanted them to. I had been well damaged physically, mentally, and emotionally when I arrived. I was whiney and felt like I was being picked on when I didn't get what I wanted. I didn't trust anyone, and lashed out when I didn't get my way. Obviously today I would be a prime candidate for counseling, but that was not available at Boys Home for me. So, I struggled through my own thoughts and behaviors, learning as I went about the world and my place in it.

But somehow, I always felt I was going to be alright in the end. I always felt protected at my core, like I was surrounded by amniotic fluid, and nothing could harm me. I believe that feeling was the beginning of my faith journey, but it took a long time for me to identify and acknowledge the source of what I felt. I had this place in my mind that I could go to when things got tough, and I grew to have a stubbornness that allowed me to plow through the rough patches I felt.

It's never been easy for me to share my feelings, with myself or others. Too scary sometimes! But I know a few things about myself that helped me through my time at Boys Home: I was not a mean person. I didn't do or say things to people to make them feel bad. I wasn't using people or a situation to get my way. I had empathy and sympathy for my brothers, although I didn't always act on it. I considered myself a good person, whatever that means.

I did lots of things I shouldn't have done and didn't do lots of things I should have done. (There has got to be an Episcopal prayer about that somewhere.) I never felt anything was owed me because of what had happened in Norfolk, and as time went on, I became fiercely proud that nothing could beat me down, that I could handle whatever life threw my way. Yes, I was cocky, often for no reason, but that feeling helped me get by. I liked people and liked to laugh, but there was something about being a Home Boy and going what I went through, that taught me to recognize bullshit when I saw it. My problem was, and this has followed me all the way through my life, I just couldn't let it go. I had to take a stand and act on what I thought was right. Sometimes it cost me, but I had to stay true to what I believed. I found I was a leader, not in a commanding way, but just being naturally me. As I have said before, the daily life and program at Boys Home was forming me, teaching me. In addition, the Sunday services at Emanuel Episcopal in Covington, and our Wednesday evening services at the chapel on campus, proved to be soothing and comforting for me over time. I wasn't serious about my faith at that point, but I did enjoy the repetitiveness of the prayer book. There was something lacking for me, although I didn't even know it or know what I was missing. It all started to come into focus in the late summer of 1960, just as I was about to start my sophomore year at CHS!

16

THE MARLBORO MAN

As I said, smoking cigarettes was a big deal across America, and smoking ads were plastered all about; magazines, billboards, radio and TV commercials, etc. One of the best advertising campaigns was for Marlboro cigarettes: the Marlboro Man. He was the strong silent type of cowboy. He was tough, stylish, affectionate, representing manliness and freedom. Paul Olen Siple didn't smoke, and the only hat I saw him wear was a baseball cap, but he became my Marlboro Man nonetheless. He was hired to coach basketball and baseball, and to help supervise the boys in the program outside of the cottages. He lived in a house on campus with his wife and two children, Beverly and Bill. Coach was forty-five years old when he moved up to The Hill with his family, and had been a teacher, coach, and principal at nearby Valley High School in Hot Springs, Virginia. He was a graduate of Bridgewater College, where he captained the baseball team, and got his Master's degree from the University of Virginia in 1957. Coach had served in the South Pacific in the Navy during World War II, but like most of that era, didn't talk about his service.

He was destined to become my role model, my father figure, and my friend. I was honored to present him for his induction into the Boys Home Hall of Fame in 2000, and to be a pallbearer at his funeral in March 2015, after he had hit the ripe old age of ninety-three.

Tenth grade started for me, and I was introduced to geometry by the one and only Maude Mahoney. I have no idea why she was in Covington or how she got to CHS, as she was a graduate of the University of Pennsylvania and Columbia University. At any rate, she was a character and a great math teacher. Like most teachers, she had extra duties, and hers was as the cafeteria manager, where she also was the cashier. Dimick and I had geometry with Maude in a classroom trailer, as the high school was going through what seemed like a major overhaul. You must picture the setup of the trailer to appreciate what happened on almost a daily basis. There were chalkboards lining the length of the walls of the trailer on one side, and our desks were in long rows facing the chalkboards. That setup put the students close to the chalkboards and close to Maude when they were at the chalkboards, working on a calculation, etc. That's because Ms. Mahoney sat in her desk right behind us in the trailer.

Every day was the same, she would call the roll by asking us in turn what got for an answer for a certain problem. If a wrong answer was given, it was always "Go to the board." That meant you worked at the blackboard until you got the problem right, with Maude kibitzing and cajoling the whole time, adding more pressure to the task. At times, there would be five or six students up there at one time. Dimick, this six-foot-one hulk of a football player, was scared of Maude, as he was often at the board for long periods of time, ducking as she called him dumb and saying he wouldn't amount to anything while throwing chalk and erasers at him.

Of course, this proved she liked him, but it took him a while to see it that way. She liked me too, but I could bob and weave with the best of them. As the semester wore on, I started figuring things out in what was called plane geometry. The first time I came through the cafeteria line with that extra piece of pie on my tray, Maude called me on it. I said, "Oh sorry, Ms. Mahoney, I'll put it back," and I did. By the fourth time I shoved that tray down the rails with that extra dessert with a smile on my face, Maude just gave me a wink as I picked my tray up and passed on by. I never wanted to take too much advantage though or put Ms. Mahoney in a spot where she would have to call me on it again, and thereafter only got that extra dessert occasionally.

Like most staff members, Coach Siple took his meals in the dining hall, and his family almost always joined him. We sat at round tables at that time, with about eight chairs at each table, so there was room for four boys to join the Siple family. The boys were normally assigned tables on a rotating basis, so it took a while for me to get my turn there. Coach wasn't a talker, at least not when he first arrived. It seemed to me that his wife did enough talking for the whole family. He was often assigned to lead some of us at rack-up after school or Saturday mornings, and I tried to make sure I got on his work crew. I wanted to get to know him better, and I sensed that he had something to offer me that I sorely needed. A boy needs a role model as he grows up. Someone he can admire and look up to, and someone who can hopefully help him become a man. I was sixteen when Paul Siple came into my life, and to that point I hadn't been lucky enough to find that man. I know a good thing when I see it, and as time went on, I saw in Coach a man I could try to emulate.

Unchained

17

LESSON LEARNED

It was early in my sophomore year and normally we took the public school bus to Covington High School, but this morning was different. All the high school boys had piled onto the Boys Home bus to be taken to the local health center for a special vaccination. Polio had ravaged the U.S. for years, with epidemics breaking out all over the place. The young were especially affected, leaving many crippled and many dead. It was very common to see young people in braces walking around on crutches. So sad. In fact, there were at least of couple of guys at Boys Home who had suffered from the disease. Jimmy Miller suffered from polio before he came up on The Hill. Jimmy was out of braces/crutches by then though.

In 1955, Dr. Jonas Salk had finished his experimental trials, and the Salk vaccine had been proven to be effective. The world literally rejoiced. Scientists had been searching for a cure for decades, and now a series of shots could provide immunity from this dreaded disease that affected the spinal cord and resulted in varying degrees of paralysis. Dr. Albert Sabin later developed a type of oral vaccine that also did the job, and I think I remember this is what we were getting that morning.

My memory is a little fuzzy on the vaccine, but not the fight. Lots of interesting things happened on the many bus rides I had while on The Hill. Usually things were pretty quiet, but with forty-five plus high school Home

Boys, things could get a little testy. Arguments and disagreements were not uncommon, and this sometimes led to fighting. Such was the case this morning.

I'm not sure how it all started, but Richard Nuckols (Nucks) and a guy named Butch Martin got into an argument and it continued as we were getting off the bus at the health clinic. We were all waiting outside as the staff member who drove the bus went inside to coordinate with the folks who worked there, while Nucks and Butch continued jawing at each other.

Now Nucks was in Greene Cottage and a proctor. He was a cool guy who played on the basketball team. He was about six feet tall, very solidly built, and a quick, good athlete. Nucks had a great personality, was good looking, and he was more than a little vain about his image. He was from Norfolk, as I was, and we were always the last two Home Boys off of the Greyhound Bus on those long rides back "home" to start vacation time at Christmas and the summer recess.

I had never seen Nuckols fight, but we all used to slap box down in the basement of Greene Cottage, and he was damn good. Well, I seldom got in on that action. I didn't want to mess up my baby face. I used to tell everybody I was a lover not a fighter. Dimick and Nuckols were always at it in a good-natured way, in between the time they were lifting free weights.

Now Nuckols prided himself on his appearance, and he was stylish. Always had a girl on his arm. The time for jawing was over, and the time for fighting was at hand. Before they started though, Nuckols calmly took off his well-pressed shirt and handed it to someone to hold, then took off his shined brown loafers and put them to one side. He said he didn't want to go into school looking sloppy.

Now Butch Martin was mean. He was from the old school at Boys Home, one of the guys who bullied others. I like to think that guys like Nuckols, Dimick, and myself helped usher in somewhat of a new era, in that we were a little gentler in our approach and leadership.

They circled around one another, and Butch threw the first punch. Nucks dodged it and smiled as Butch missed again. Nuckols was left-handed and he started peppering Butch's nose with right jabs in the classic boxing style. Jab, move, jab, move, etc. Butch was flailing, and it wasn't long before he began to realize that he had made a big mistake. He couldn't back down right away in front of everyone, however, and tried to go on the defensive to protect himself. Nuckols played with him a little while longer and then—Boom, Boom, Boom, Boom! Right jab. Powerful left hook. Right hook. Left hook. Over!

Blood trickled from Butch's nose when Nuckols hit him with that pretty combination. Just like that, the fight was over.

Without saying a word, Nucks reached for his shirt, buttoned it up, and put his loafers back on. Butch hadn't touched him. As usual, the staff member who had driven the bus reappeared just after the fight was over. Pete Felty was a former Home Boy, and he let the altercation play out. Most of the time, two willing fighters were left to sort it out for themselves. There was a lesson to be learned: Keep your mouth shut unless you are willing to back your words up.

Unchained

18

VARSITY BASKETBALL '60–'61

Basketball tryouts couldn't come soon enough. Of course, all the guys spent some time in the gym trying to hone their skills, but I was spending all my free time there. I loved the game to the point of obsession. Dimick and Pete Davis were still playing football for the Cougars, so they were relegated to working on their hoop skills on the weekends.

Finally, it was time for tryouts! We were going to be a young team. The previous year's varsity had a good season, but almost all those players had graduated. In fact, the only returner was a senior named Roy Hedges, and he was not a starter the previous year. He had a nickname, "Slur," and I'll let you guess why. Slur was a pretty good guy and an average player, but a tough competitor. Tryouts were brutal. Coach basically ran our butts off, establishing right away who was in charge, and let us know this was serious business. In the past we had played zone defense, but Coach Siple had us practicing a pressing man-to-man defense, with a fast-breaking offense to score quickly. I found out Coach might not have much to say around the campus, but he had plenty to say, and loudly, in the gym.

I do believe that is where I picked up my habit of breaking clipboards years later when I was coaching, as Coach Siple destroyed a few that winter. We were an extremely competitive bunch, and there were more than a few times when Coach had to separate guys for fighting. There were no returning starters, so everyone was trying to catch Coach's eye, but eventually we settled into a rotation. With such a young team learning a new system, we struggled early on, but then hit our stride and won our last few games. We finished the season 12-5, and the future looked bright for the Hilltopper hoopsters. I finished my first varsity season leading the team with seventeen points per game and was the second leading rebounder.

One thing I learned early was that individual achievements were secondary to what the team did: That we all depend on each other. That it is the responsibility of each teammate to lift the others up. That no player is trying to screw up intentionally. Coach taught these truths in both overt and subtle ways, as each individual situation presented itself as a teachable moment.

At one of our first practices, he used me to make a point. He had everyone go sit in our small group of bleachers, and then called me out onto the floor. He put a basketball in my hand and said, and I'm paraphrasing here, "We all know Nunnally is a good scorer, but he needs all of you to help him to put the ball in the basket." Then he told me to go to the baseline, step out of bounds, and pass the ball inbounds.

I walked out of bounds, a little confused, and said, "There's no one to pass the ball to and I can't pass it in to myself." "Exactly" came the reply. In this teaching he had made me feel good about my talents, by calling me out onto the floor to help demonstrate, but at the same time made me and the rest of the team realize we were dependent on each other. After practice I waited until Coach was by himself, and I asked with a smiling face, "Coach, can't I just grab a rebound, dribble to the other end of the court, and score?" He put his index finger to his smiling lips and walked away.

As I said earlier, in Coach Siple I had found the man I had been missing my entire life. He wasn't complicated, and you always knew where you stood with him. He was a fierce competitor and wanted to win, and he taught us how to win and lose with dignity and class. He had a sense of right and wrong that resonated with me, and he stuck to his principles. It didn't matter who you were, if you crossed that line, Coach would call you on it, and then put you back on the straight and narrow. He pretty much always did this in a matter-of-fact way, never raising his voice or showing his ire, which wasn't the case with all the staff.

Coach never played favorites, and treated the general population just the way he treated his ballplayers, even handed and firmly. As for the basketball and baseball teams, he treated all the players and managers alike. But sometimes I felt like Dimick and I caught extra grief just so Coach could say he wasn't playing favorites. I spent as much time around him as I could, trying to soak up his knowledge and his good vibe. We didn't see much of his wife except at mealtimes, but I liked his daughter, Bev, and his young son, Bill. Bev was a good-looking girl two years behind me in school, and we became friends. Years later she also attended Bridgewater College, and she ended up marrying my best friend and roommate, Jim Ellis.

Coach was just as much a competitor and loved to win as we were, and this story proves it!

Coach Siple had scheduled us to play a basketball game at Beaumont, an institution for juvenile offenders located outside of Richmond, Virginia. It was basically for criminals under the age of eighteen. Those who were too young to incarcerate with adult men. We had loaded on our bus sometime after breakfast that Saturday morning for the 160-mile trip to the game. The trip took over three hours in the time before interstates had reached that part of Virginia.

It was a small group, as Coach usually carried just ten players and a manager. We passed our time in the usual way, talking, singing, gambling, and, on long trips such as this, sleeping. This was well before the time of the boom box, Walkman, or iPod, and so we had to keep ourselves entertained. Coach Siple drove the bus and usually let us just be ourselves, as long as it didn't get too rowdy. After the long ride from The Hill, we got off the bus, walked around a little bit to stretch our legs, and then headed to their dining hall for an early lunch—our pre-game meal.

We were sitting and eating at a table separate from the others when the Beaumont boys came into the dining hall for their lunch. They lined up single file, with their hands clasped behind their back. They looked straight ahead, and were not allowed to talk, even to the point of having to nod to the servers to indicate whether they wanted a certain food. They all wore the same brown uniforms, and one of them turned to and said something to the guy behind him. That's when he got knocked to the ground. We saw the guard hit him a couple of times with the nightstick and he went to the ground, balling himself up into the fetal position. The guard then kicked him a couple of times, then stepped back. The boy got up, put his hands behind his back, and looked straight ahead. The scary part for me? The boy made never made a sound!

Game time came and we got dressed and went into the gym for warm-ups. They had a very vocal crowd, and soon they started calling me "baby face" every time I touched the ball. No big deal for me. In fact, that kind of stuff always got me more motivated and focused. The game started, and they are bad. We jumped out early on them, and it just got worse for them as the game went on. They had only one player who was any good at all, and he was a hothead who couldn't control his temper. He spent most of his time yelling at the refs, his own players, and his coach. By halftime it was something like 36-8. Of course, Coach was trying to hold the score down, but except for that one guy, everyone on our team was better than any player they had. When we went in for halftime and Coach Siple is telling us to keep a cool head and not let the fans get to us. We had a good laugh when we heard the hothead had quit his team and turned in his uniform before the start of the third quarter. We finished the game without any more issues.

Fast forward to the spring, and we are back at Beaumont for a baseball game. (I don't think we played them in anything except for that one year.) I was pitching for our side, and guess who took the mound for them. Yep, it was the hothead. As with basketball, he was their only good player, but we couldn't believe what we saw when we went to bat in the top of the first inning. This kid could bring the heat with his fastball! He had a great arm and could throw fast—the fastest I had seen to that point. In addition, he had a pretty good curveball. He definitely was looking forward to this rematch with us. He kept his cool despite our trying to rag on him, and he dominated our bats. I think we beat them 2-1 or 3-1, but mostly we scored because of errors or walks, not because we could touch the pitcher.

They had an inmate in the stands right by third base who was razing our third baseman, Pete Davis. "Greasy" was giving it right back to him, then some of their other fans started getting rowdy. Coach Siple was just about to hand out the bats when the guards settled them down. The game ended without further incident, and we headed back to Covington, talking about how good that pitcher was.

Late that summer, just before school was to start, I realized that I was now going to be the number two pitcher and number one first baseman on the baseball team my junior year. How did I know that? The hothead, Buddy Hobbs, had become a Boys Home Boy! As we later learned, Coach Siple had basically recruited Buddy, and had convinced the Director, Chief Burrowes, to give him a chance. Coach loved to win. Buddy became one of my best friends, and he added greatly to our lives on The Hill, in sports and in other ways. He could still show his temper at times, but he learned to keep it under wraps for the most part. He was eventually drafted by the Phillies and played minor league ball. I heard he became a Pastor later in life, and I'm sure that there was some great music in that church, as Buddy had a sweet, sweet voice. He led us in many call and response spirituals on future bus trips.

Boys Home has had its share of miraculous stories, and I've got to share this one with you now. Donnie got caught stealing nine silver dollars, was arrested, and soon became a "ward of the state." There were two other boys who were involved in the theft, and Donnie got three bucks as his share. It was a small town, and naturally people wondered where those two young boys had gotten the silver dollars they were spending. Donnie didn't even get to spend his ill-gotten gains before he was caught! Of course, that wasn't his first offense, as he had been caught stealing ice cream earlier, and had been running the mean streets of Clintwood, Virginia for some time.

Donnie lived up a "holler" about a mile outside of this small coal town with his mother, sister and three brothers. They shared the twenty-by-thirty–foot "house" with his grandmother, who owned the property. Donnie's mom had not married at that point, and worked in town in what was called a restaurant but was more of a beer joint. She worked long shifts six days a week, and often didn't see her kids awake on a daily basis, especially when they were in school.

Clintwood was a tough little town, and Donnie learned early on how to handle himself. His mom told him not to start any fights, but she admonished him that if he got into a fight, to finish it. After his grandmother died, the family moved into town to be closer to the schools and his mom's job. They bounced around a bit, never staying in one place for too long.

Donnie's transgressions landed him in Richmond for three to four months, and when he arrived on The Hill in 1959, he was twelve years old. Like many of the new arrivals, there was an adjustment period for Donnie, and he chafed against the yoke of a structured life. He hit the road once as a runaway, got three licks and no supper from Pete Felty, a former Home Boy who had returned as a staff member. He decided after that to try and stay with the program. After a couple of years in Jack Gordon Cottage, and a failed attempt in Sam's Cottage, Donnie hit the jackpot by being transferred to Greene Cottage for his eighth grade year.

He will tell you that he got strong leadership from Dimick and me, and gentle, yet firm care from Granny that helped many a boy over the years. There was one thing everyone learned quickly about Donnie, and that was not to mess with him. He was a tough little nut. He was all boy, and quickly got involved in all kinds of activities on The Hill. He was serious about Scouting, (unlike me), played football and ran track at Covington High

School and Allegheny High School, and played for Boys Home on our basketball team. I have a team picture of the Hilltoppers, Dimick's and my senior year, and there is Donnie, a freshman, sitting stern-like as one of our managers.

Chief Burrowes, the Director of Boys Home, would often have one-on-one time with the boys to assess where they were in school and campus life, and to help them make plans for their future. He guided Donnie into thinking about college, even though no one from Donnie's family had ever graduated from high school. By the end of his junior year at Allegheny High School, Donnie had excelled in the classroom and was leader on the Boys Home campus. Like Dimick and me before him, Donnie was Chief's sidekick on trips to help raise money for Boys Home, and Donnie met some folks who were strong on the program at Virginia Military Institute. A couple of them were on the Boys Home Board of Trustees, and they were pushing Chief Burrowes to get a Boys Home Boy to go there. Mr. Burrowes had talked to me about VMI, but we went there to see a football game once, and after I saw how the "Rats" (first year students) were treated, I told Chief that was not the place for me!

Donnie arrived there as a freshman Rat in the fall of 1966, and as a true Boys Home Boy, quickly learned how to navigate the system without drawing too much attention to himself, and at the same time, doing just enough to get the job done.

There was an exception however: His junior year as a cadet saw a minor incident escalate into a situation that almost led to his dismissal. Basically, he saw something that was a little sketchy going on, made a comment on it, and then wouldn't back down when "the authorities" tried to push him into a corner. Donnie got arrested for the weekend and was sent to the Commanding General, who dressed him down and made him feel about one inch tall. He did this by reminding Donnie of all the people who helped him get into VMI, and who were looking for Donnie to validate their trust in him.

What Donnie didn't learn until later though, was that Coach Siple had secretly come to the campus and gone to bat for him with the General. That was just like Coach Siple, always working behind the scenes for one of the boys, especially his players. Donnie graduated with an engineering degree in the morning of a pretty significant day in 1970, as he married his high school sweetheart, Mary, that evening! (Mary was one of the Heavenly Angels sent here on earth, and she returned to heaven a few years ago). After a year of grad school at Virginia Tech, and a three-year stint in the Marines, Donnie landed a job with Proctor and Gamble, first working in Pennsylvania and then in Georgia. Meanwhile Mary and Donnie became parents of two boys, and settled into the middle class life.

In 1984, Donnie was looking for a challenge and moved back to Covington to work for Westvaco, a paper mill that was the largest employer in the area. Donnie had come full circle, a testament to his hard work, strong moral character, and the support of so many along the way. Boys Home had changed his life!

Oh, I forgot to mention his last name: Wheatley. Donnie Wheatley, the boy who turned into a man, who then dedicated his life into turning other troubled boys into men. Donnie Wheatley, who answered the call in 1985 to become the leader of the institution that had supported and nurtured him. Donnie Wheatley, the Director of Boys Home from 1985 to December 2021. He did an outstanding job at the helm of Boys Home for the over thirty-five years, guiding the boys and staff with a firm and loving hand through a significant time of positive transition. Donnie, I am proud and honored to call you friend, and I'm sorry for all those times I hit you with a coat hanger to get you out of bed in the morning.

19

JUST CRUISING ALONG

The fall of 1961 brought me back to Covington High School for my Junior year. It had been a good summer with vacations to New Jersey to visit my sister, Ceal, and her family, and of course to Norfolk for another two-week vacation with the Walkers. It was so important to me to have these two families in my life, but we didn't share the same intimacy as a normal family. And I missed that—although at that time I couldn't name it or identify the "something" that was lacking in my life. I know teens are notorious for keeping their worries and fears to themselves, but just to know there is someone to talk to about romance and the future, and to ask "Am I normal?", would have been comforting.

Of course, there was a lot of talking about girls in the basement! Everybody had their opinions, but honestly it was mostly based on anything but experience! I do remember a funny interaction Pete and I had working rack-up one afternoon. We were working with Jake Cleek, and Redeye asked him how he got so lucky to marry Mrs. Cleek, as she was a very attractive woman. Not waiting for an answer, he then asked Jake what advice he would give for a guy wanting to marry. Jake, who was a short, stout man with a husky voice, laughed and said, "Hoss, pick a lean horse for a long race!" We all laughed, but it sure made sense to me.

The only sex talk I got at Boys Home was short and to the point. We had just started basketball tryouts for my junior year, and the Varsity and JV hopefuls had just gotten on the floor and were shooting around. But the conversation we were having wasn't about hoops, it was about a missing player. Jimmy wasn't at practice, and we had all heard what had happened to him. He was a sophomore and had been dating this girl from Covington for a few months. They had started having sex and Jimmy was telling everyone on The Hill about it. Not only that, he had notched a piece of wood for every time they had "done the deed."

Well, he had broken up with her recently and she was mad about it, so she told her folks what they had been doing. The result was that Jimmy was being sent to Beaumont Correctional Center as she was underage. Coach Siple walked into the gym and called us all over to the bleachers. As we sat down it was obvious by the look on his face that this was going to be a serious talk. He said, "Boys, I know you all have heard what happened to Jimmy. The only thing I can tell you is to keep it in your pants." That phrase was repeated over and over for the next couple of weeks! It was just so much fun to say. I sure never had to worry about that while I was on The Hill.

I had finally started dating someone on a regular basis though. Her name was Faye Reynolds, and she was a cutie. One great thing about Faye was that she had a car! Well, she had access to her family car, and that was a game changer for me. On town nights, she would come pick me up, so I didn't have to hitchhike into town—and of course I became even more popular with the guys we could take in with us.

We would often take in a movie or go to home football games, but mostly we would hang out at her house. Her folks were nice, down to earth, and we could go to her room for some privacy from her younger sister. Faye was the first girl I ever made out with, and that would set me into a frenzy! Faye liked kissing too, but she was good at fending off my roaming hands, and a stern "No" kept me in line.

I didn't have to worry about hitchhiking back to The Hill, and we almost always took some guys with their thumbs out at the Esso station back with us. We would drop them off, then pull into a quiet spot near the admin building, and make out until it was time for me check in. I'm telling you, those car windows sure could get steamy during the winter.

Covington had a local newspaper that reported on all the high school sports, and Faye would cut out all the stories about the Boys Home Hilltoppers. It was great to see my name in print, that winter, but I know we were not seeing each other in the spring, because I have no newspaper clippings about baseball! One of our last dates was the Valentine's Dance. There were lots dances at CHS; we had Homecoming, Sadie Hawkins (where the girls asked the boys) Christmas Dance, Junior/Senior Prom, and sometimes we just had sock hops.

I loved music and dancing and would sing everywhere I went. In '62, *The Twist* by Chubby Checker was big—both the song and the new dance craze! Of course, we danced to the jitterbug, but it was always fun to see how fast the dance floor filled up when a slow song was played. There were lots of instrumental hits, and I recall a couple that I really liked: *Stranger on the Shore* and *Last Date*. Slow dancing was romantic. As I recall, Faye had caught me slow dancing real close with another girl, and her reaction was basically, "Don't let the door hit you in the butt on the way out!" It was tough having to hitchhike back and forth to town again.

That Junior year, Dimick and I took typing together. Chief Burrowes had suggested that we take typing, which would come in handy if we went to college. College? Had anyone in my family had ever gone to college, was I destined to be the first one? I didn't know because I didn't know anything about my family, aside from my sister. Sometimes I felt like I was an island unto myself. Who the hell was I anyway? Where was I headed? Luckily, I fell asleep quickly every night, and I didn't have time during the day to focus on anything serious, so I just went along dealing with the day to day.

That's what Boys Home was good at: providing stability, teaching us to do the right thing, over and over, day by day. So, at that time, who was I? I was a Boys Home Boy and a ballplayer. But even then, although I didn't know it, there was more. I had sympathy and empathy for the underdog, for people who were thought of by many as less than or "other." I mean, that was me too, wasn't it?

Pete and I had Ms. Beulah Jones for typing, in what they then called the Practical Arts. You guessed it, we were in a trailer. Beulah sat at one end, and there were two rows of typing tables and chairs on each side.

Typing is practice, practice, practice, and we had a typewriter in the cottage we could use. But for me, practicing typing was way down on my priority list, right behind shining my shoes. Actually, I always shined my school shoes, but often just before I put them on to head down for the bus. For Dimick, typing was even further down the list. We had the old style manual typewriter, where you had to pound the keys to be able to read the type correctly.

A big part of our grade were the timed tests we took quite often. In these, Beulah would have a timer, and we would all type the same assignment until the bell rang. We were graded on how many words we could type in a certain amount of time, say a minute, with points taken off for mistakes. Dimick sat right behind me in the last row on one side, and he would often continue typing when the bell sounded. Ms. Jones would holler at him, and he would say something like, "I'm almost finished Ms. Jones." Everyone in the class would laugh, and Pete would smile broadly.

I noticed early on in the semester we took the course that Ms. Jones was saving Blue Horse labels, and she had a coupon redeemer booklet that let her know what you could redeem. This was another big redeeming business, like S & H Green Stamps. Blue Horse paper was big in those days, and that's what we got from Boys Home to use in school. They sold all different kinds of paper, including typing paper. There was a picture of a blue horse on every wrapper, with a point value depending on the price of the paper. You could use the points to redeem things from the catalog. Beulah Jones, bless her, was to me the epitome of what we would think of as an old spinster. I'm not sure if she was married though. It seemed to me as if she wore that same plain blue dress constantly.

I told Dimick we should help her get Blue Horse wrappers, and after letting the typing class know they should give her all their wrappers, we really got down to business. If we saw anyone in school open a pack of paper, we would take their wrapper and make them promise to save all others for us going forward. It didn't take long until we were Knights of the Blue Horse! Once we got a nice pile of them, we would stop by after class and discreetly put them on Beulah's desk, making sure she saw us of course. We were hoping for a better grade. She would thank us while shyly turning her head away. I credit that typing class for keeping me out of the jungles of Vietnam. When I enlisted in the Army in 1966, I was able to be assigned as a clerk instead of an infantryman, because of my ability to type.

Dimick had started to lift weights seriously and it was showing! He was probably six feet tall, 220 pounds his Junior year, and was dominating at offensive guard and defensive end. Pete was good-natured most of the time, but nobody wanted to cross him. The Covington Cougar football team was off to a very good start in the Blue Ridge District, and a big game was coming up at Cave Spring High School, near Roanoke, Virginia. I couldn't get a ride over there to watch the game, but listened on the radio as we tied them 6-6, ending their twelve-game winning streak!

As it turns out, in a freak season that saw them tie in two other games, the next year when they came to play us at home, they then had an eighteen-game winning streak! We were undefeated also, so the game promised to be a donnybrook! Our small stadium was packed with fans as they had brought several charter buses full of fans to the game. They had a very good lineman named Sands Woody, and our coaching had been priming Dimick, who was now up to 230 pounds, telling him Woody was the better player. The donnybrook never happened, as we destroyed them 34-0, and Redeye destroyed Sands Woody!

When basketball season rolled around my junior year, Coach Siple had his hands full trying to curb our expectations, as we knew we had a lot of talent coming back, having lost only one player from the team that was 12-5 last year. That loss of Slur was more than offset by the addition of Buddy Hobbs from Beaumont!. We were goofing around the first day of practice, and, for the first time ever, I witnessed Coach break a clipboard in practice. He called us to the bleachers and told us we hadn't won anything yet. Unlike the previous year when he had built me up early on, he dressed me out, telling everyone he was considering making someone else the team captain. That put me in my place pretty quick, and Coach never had to admonish me for anything about sports again. He simmered us down by running the ever-loving hell out of us for the first two weeks, with a promise of more to come if we didn't practice up to his expectations!

Coach knew we would be up for the games, but to get better as the season wore on, we had to focus during practice. In a bit of a surprise for me, Richard Knuckles had improved his game, and early on in practice showed excellent defensive ability. He was in his post-graduate year at CHS, having finished the eleventh grade and graduated the previous June. He was seriously dating a girl in town, and I think he stayed just so he could be around her. He was around five feet, eleven inches tall, muscular, and quick as a cat. A tenacious defender and rebounder for his size. After he left Boys Home in 1962, "Nucks" joined the Air Force, and in 1965 was a Bronze Medal winner at the FIBT World Championships competing in the four-man bobsled event in St. Moritz, Switzerland. Not too shabby!

We started strong on the hardwood and were undefeated as we started preparing for the Christmas holiday season. I had straightened my attitude out and was made the captain, which with so many leader types on this team, was just an honorary title. Playing with guys who were like brothers to you, and who were excellent athletes and players in their own right, led to a respect for each other you wouldn't often see on a high school team.

Buddy Hobbs was the new guy and a good player, but he tended to be a bit of a showboat. Pete and I were talking about it one night in the cottage and he said, "I'll take care of it." The next day at practice, Pete found the right time to get in Buddy's face for showboating, and Buddy made the mistake of talking back to Dimick. He got smacked hard in the face for his troubles, and from then on, all Dimick had to do was remind him that he could get smacked at any time. Personally, I was on a roll, and the newspaper writers became infatuated with my foul shooting and reported on it every game. I was shooting well, though, and at one point hit fifteen in a row. Here's a little snippet from the write-up with our game with Boiling Springs, a small high school near Covington.

> The Boys Home Hilltoppers had very little trouble in gaining their 15th consecutive win as they trounced Boiling Springs by a 67-21 count. The Hilltoppers used two full units with each team playing equal time with all but one man breaking into the scoring act. Mike Nunnally led the attack with 13 points and has sunk 15 free shots in 15 tries in the last three games.

Coach was killing my per game average by only letting the first unit play half of some of the blow-out games!

Unchained

20

THE VIRGIN GRANNY

It was nearing Christmas vacation and we laughed and said to Granny, "There's no way you are a virgin!"

All the boys in Greene Cottage were in the living room (that was a crowd in that small room!) with our housemother planning what we were going to do for our Christmas decorations this year. Every year around Christmas we would all pitch in and help decorate the cottage. We had some lights and a few other things, but we also had to be creative to get a good look. Guys would get pinecones and paint them silver or white, string cranberries or popcorn for the tree, get pine branches to decorate the mantel, etc. Just doing the kind of stuff many families would do before the age of plastic and Chinese imports.

Of course, we also found time to fill out our Christmas wish list. I think I remember we would sometimes have a check off list that we could use to help let people know what we wanted. We never knew exactly what happened to the list, but usually I got at least one specific thing that I had asked for. Boys Home would send out an appeal to its list of donors and sponsors to help with the cost of buying gifts for all the boys, and people would respond with either cash donations or actual gifts. It was basic, and I pretty much always asked for clothes. We would open our gifts just before we left the campus to go to our "homes" for Christmas vacation. It was an exciting time, and there would be some trading of gifts, and sometimes a bit of jealousy.

Now you must remember that we made just about everything into a competition, but for the cottage decorations, there was already a contest built in. Every year, the ladies from the local Covington auxiliary or garden club would drive out and judge our efforts.

Greene Cottage wanted to be the best at everything, so there were lots of ideas being tossed out about how we could impress the judges and win this thing again. Someone came up with the idea of having a Nativity scene, and then somebody else made it a brilliant idea by suggesting we make it a "live" Nativity scene. Suddenly the creative juices got flowing, and we had the physical logistics of the stable figured out.

All the guys were saying what they wanted to be, shepherds, wise men, animals, etc. So, Pete and I made a command decision. He would be Joseph and I would be one of the Wise Men. He punched me when I told him that made the most sense, as I was smarter than he was! The other boys called dibs on this and that and pretty soon we were all set. The costumes were basically bathrobes, T-shirts, and towels—and scrounge anything else we could find. Jesus would be a doll from one the staff member's kids, naked but wrapped in a towel—swaddling clothes.

Somebody said, "Wait, who's going to be the Virgin Mary? All eyes turned to "Granny," our housemother! Now Granny was a little shy, so she tried to decline her opportunity to be on center stage. After much pleading and cajoling from "her boys," she finally gave in. Then the laughing and joking started. "Granny, how can you be the Virgin Mary when you have kids and grandkids?" We were literally rolling on the living room floor, laughing at the thought.

Well, we got everything built and put together, and held a couple of rehearsals before the big judging. We admonished the other cottages not to try and copy us, because we knew we had a winner! And we did. The ladies loved it, and Granny ended up loving her role. With *Silent Night* playing softly in the background, we acted out our parts with outer reverence and inward giggles, and there were a few wet eyes in the crowd.

Frances "Granny" Myers, from nearby Clifton Forge, came to Boys Home and Greene Cottage in 1960. She retired in 1976 and passed at the ripe old age of ninety-one. Granny was much beloved and was inducted into the Boys Home Hall of Fame.

Unchained

21

LESSONS AND SPORTSMANSHIP

A couple of days later, I learned a very hard lesson. I was not a very good pool player or gambler. A few boys had been dropped off at the Greyhound bus station in Covington, tickets in hand, for the ride home for Christmas vacation. As there were different times and schedules for various destinations, I found I had about a ninety-minute wait for my bus headed East to Norfolk. Normally Knuckles would be riding with me, but he had gotten permission to leave a few days early. Roger "Cornbread" Mays, who was from Lynchburg, was also going to have to wait for over an hour for his bus, so we headed across the street to the pool hall to kill some time.

Cornbread was the boy who kept the gym clean, so we were well acquainted with each other. He was on the JV basketball team, and with all that time spent in the gym, had become a good outside shooter. The pool game of choice was always eight-ball, and as "Bread" racked them up, I said, "What are we playing for"? He surprised me when he said, "a quarter," for that was big money to a Home Boy in those days. I had played with him before, so I knew his game wasn't as good as mine, so I said "OK" as I hammered the cue ball.

We went back and forth for a while, and it was obvious that Cornbread had gotten better since the last time I played him. There was a pool table in the basement of his cottage, so he had chances to practice that I didn't have. The clock was ticking on the wall, with only about twenty minutes until my bus was to arrive, and I was already down a buck fifty. I needed to get my money back quickly, so I offered to double the bet. That was a big mistake! In short order I had lost all my money, and it was time for the day-long bus ride to Norfolk, with no money for food or drink. I asked Cornbread for a loan, but he refused, and I had just enough time to grab my bag and board the bus before it pulled out.

I was a hungry, thirsty, tired puppy when I arrived in Norfolk, but I had caught a big break as Burley Walker was there to pick me up. He said his truck was being repaired so he wasn't on the road until tomorrow. I didn't tell him about the pool game, but explained I had no money, and I thanked him profusely when he slipped that ten-spot into my hand. My pool playing became for fun only from that day forward, but Cornbread was going to pay a price for refusing to loan me cash for the trip.

Christmastime with the Walkers was always fun. We didn't do squat for Christmas on 34th Street with my mother and stepfather. Etta ran the show, and there were certain traditions that had to be followed. Of course, the Baptist church played a big role in the festivities, but the tree couldn't be put up until Christmas Eve. Aluminum Christmas trees were popular, with the foil needles illuminated from below by a rotating color wheel. None of that nonsense for the Walkers—it had to be a live tree, with all blue lights. There was lots of silver tinsel to be put on the tree, hung one strand at a time. No throwing or clumping.

I was older now, in high school, with a little more discerning taste in clothes, and Etta made sure to let me pick out a couple of things that were in style. A far cry from the Leggett in Covington where the Home Boys shopped.

The Christmas Eve service at Foxhall was nice, but the Baptists didn't sing *O Come, O Come, Emanuel* like the Episcopalians did.

Tommy was home from VPI, and on a Saturday morning he said he was going to play pick-up basketball at Norview High School and asked me if I wanted to come along. I couldn't get my workout stuff and sneakers on any faster. Tommy was a good athlete who played three sports at Norview, and he seemed to know everybody in the gym. There were all ages there, but mostly college-age guys. Nobody knew me, so for the first couple of games I was relegated to the side baskets playing two-on-two or three-on-three.

The team Tommy was on had won a couple of games, and I was watching them out of the corner of my eye. One of the guys on his team rolled an ankle and couldn't continue, so Tommy called me over and asked if I wanted to play. Oh, Did I! I got knocked around a bit as I was a skinny six foot-three, but the other team made the mistake of letting me shoot. Of course, there was no three-point line in those days, but I connected on a few deep ones, and sank a couple of my patented hook shoots. Then they tightened up the defense on the baby-faced kid.

After the last game, a man came over and started asking me about myself. Turns out he was one of the basketball coaches at Norview, and he was impressed with my game. That was nice, and on the ride home later, Tommy told me the coach had spoken to him about me. Tommy explained my situation, that I was living in a home for boys, and said the coach wondered if I would like to transfer to Norview for the second semester and play for them. Now Norview was a big AAA high school, and I would be playing on a better team with better opponents. But I never gave it a second thought as I told Tommy I loved where I was and loved my brothers.

I was a Boys Home Boy for life!

Our basketball exploits continued apace after the Christmas break, and we got a new boy in Greene Cottage. We called him "tons of fun," "fat baby" and all sorts of other names because we cared for him, and yes, in our own unstated way, because we loved him. He was one of our brothers. His name was Jimmy Miller. He came to Boys Home in 1959, and moved into Greene Cottage in 1962.

Jimmy had been in a home for crippled children at one time because he had contracted polio when he was very young, and his hip had not grown correctly. In addition to his limp, he was overweight. We didn't cut him any slack, however. Dimick used to make Jimmy go into the bathroom with only his shorts on and make Jimmy look at himself in the mirror. Then Dimick would say, "What are you going to do about that?"

I know that sounds really harsh and cruel today, but I think subconsciously us Home Boys all knew that as underdogs in the world, we would have to be tough to make it out there. So, we pushed each other, and it wasn't always pretty. It was competition, competition, competition. We had never heard of the term self-esteem, and in fact we would have probably laughed at it. In our world you had to earn your status, and no one was praised just to make them feel better. Jimmy had been cut too much slack for too long. Pete and I got on him so much he used to hide from us.

Because of our mindset, we had some great athletes on The Hill, and we all wanted to be that Alpha Male. Luckily, we had a great Coach in Paul Siple. He helped keep us grounded. He was always pushing us to get better, to do it the right way, to make the most of our God-given abilities. No " prima donnas" were allowed.

Coach Siple, by his example, taught me many things that I carried over into my life and into my teaching and coaching career. One of the lessons was that you never embarrass your opponents by running up the score. There is nothing to be gained by humiliating the other team. In both my junior and senior years, we were very dominant in basketball. In '61–'62, we were 14-3, and in '62–'63, we ended the year 18-1, with our only loss at the hands of Bridgewater College's Freshman Team. In many games, the outcome would be settled by mid-way through the second quarter. We would have a big lead, and Coach Siple would substitute all the starters out, and the second string would finish the first half.

After halftime, the starters would be put back in, and depending on the score, we might play the entire third quarter. After that, if we had a big lead, say fifteen points or so, we knew we were done for the night. Of course, that philosophy kept our team scoring average, and my per game average down, but I came to accept it and to even be proud of how we conducted ourselves. This attitude toward not running up the score was prevalent in that day and time. I even knew of football coaches who, when their team had a big lead in the fourth quarter, would only play defense for the rest of the game. If they got the ball back, they would punt the ball to the other team on first down to prevent any more scores by their team. Unfortunately, that level of sportsmanship has disappeared from our fields and courts.

By the time we were seniors, Pete and I realized we were big fish in a little pond, and our mantra became, "Whatcha gonna do after high school?" This was said in our best thick "country" accent, and we must have asked each other this question on an almost daily basis. This little saying helped keep us focused, and indeed later we both found a path forward to success.

What about "fat baby"? Jimmy Miller changed his body, lifted weights, and played football, wrestled, and participated in track in high school. He played football at Ferrum Junior College, and graduated from East Tennessee State University. Not bad, "tons of fun."

We were on the bus headed to play with our 18-game winning streak on the line. This was not one of the patsy teams though, we were going to play against the Bridgewater College JV team. This game would not be allowed had we been a normal public high school team, but we were playing as an independent school. We were excited for the game, but wondered how we would fare against men. It was still daylight when we arrived, and we headed straight to their cafeteria for a pre-game meal. We thought we had hit the big time. Bridgewater had a pretty campus, and we took a short walk around before heading to the gym for the game. We were going to play the preliminary game before the varsity contest. It was the biggest gym any of us had played in, but still had a cozy atmosphere. The Bridgewater Eagles were a Division III school of about twelve hundred students, and played in the Mason-Dixon Conference.

My palms were sweating, and my throat was dry as Coach gave us a pre-game talk. He was trying to convey that this was just another game, but I knew that wasn't the case. Our guys were all intimidated as we started our lay-up drill, and when our opponents took the floor to start their warm-up routine, we all turned to watch them. Coach Siple called us over and told us to concentrate on what we were doing, but it was too late. The game was essentially over before it had started!

We were outmatched from the start, and at halftime were bickering among each other, as we were not used to being down by double digits. Coach calmed us down by saying he was proud of us, and that we played hard. As we took the floor to warm up for the second half, he pulled me aside and said I needed to step up my scoring. I nodded and went to work, ending the game with eighteen points. We had cut their lead to 41-36 at the end of the third quarter, but they killed us on the boards in the final quarter and ran away with the game. As a team, we were totally dejected as we sat in the bleachers watching the varsity game. I don't remember who won, but I do remember being excited at the thought that I might one day be a college player.

We went into a funk after the loss to Bridgewater, and, as a result, lost two of our last three games. One of those losses was in overtime to a school in Pennsylvania, where we had spent a day and night before the game. I wasn't ready to play, only scored seventeen, and we got beat in overtime. The Hilltoppers still ended up 14-3, had bragging rights as the best team in the area, and we had learned a valuable lesson for the future: Don't let defeat in life bring you down and make the future worse. Everybody loses some, but the key is to pick yourself up off the ground and keep grinding toward your goal.)

I was maintaining a decent grade point average in school, but I just didn't have the drive and self-discipline to fully do my best. I wasn't alone in that regard for sure, and I was happy just getting by. I had a few friends at CHS, but no one I was close with except Temple Kessinger. He was a good friend of Pete's who also played football, and our senior year we called ourselves the Three Musketeers. It was an odd situation for Home Boys as we weren't available to do anything after school with friends during the week and had no transportation for the weekends. I did enjoy our youth group at Emanuel Episcopal, and we had a couple of outings to Grace Episcopal in Lexington that were fun, but mostly we were a closed community. Except for the ladies of course!

Buddy Hobbs did become our number one pitcher in the spring of '62, and he was 8-0 on the season. I played first base and was 3-0 on the mound. "Cornbread" also won one game. Knuckles, Dimick, Bobby Davidson, and Pete Davis, all basketball players on that 14-3 team, helped lead us to the 12-0 record. Melvin Dove, a senior who played only baseball, was our second baseman and Captain. Coach Siple was a real baseball man, and his brother, Claude, who had played pro for a while, would often come up and help us with our skill development.

That summer Coach managed the American Legion baseball team, and I joined Pete and Buddy on that team. We were loaded! Dimick was our catcher, Buddy played left field when not pitching, and I was a sub who pitched occasionally and pinch hit. We were joined by a group of Cougars who were also good players. Gary Rice, shortstop, John Mills, center field, and the best pitcher on our team, Billy Hepler.

Billy was drafted after his senior year and played one season in the Major Leagues for the New York Mets. He was a great guy, six-foot-one, 160 pounds, and skinny as a rail.

We were getting ready to play the Roanoke Legion team at Cave Spring High School, just outside of Roanoke, Virginia. As usual, Coach Siple drove his station wagon to the game, and Dimick and I rode with him, with the game site over an hour's drive away. Buddy had somehow missed the departure time, and Coach was old school, not even giving him an extra five-minute leeway. When it came time to leave, we left. It was such a great opportunity for me to get to spend some quality time with the man I most respected, admired, and loved. The three of us talked and bantered back and forth, mostly about baseball, but really just about anything that came into our vision or into our minds. Coach Siple always had a pocketful of wisdom to dispense, in an easy, matter-of-fact way. One of his favorites was "for a nickel more you can go first class," which was his way of saying don't do things on the cheap, it was worth paying a little more for a quality experience or a quality product. That stuck with me.

We had taken our warm-ups, and I trotted out to start out in left field because Buddy wasn't there. Typically, I would be our number three pitcher, and would be a sub at first base or the outfield. It was a nice playing on this field all right, but it had one major flaw. The field was laid out so that when the sun set in the summer, it was directly into the batter's eyes. Not a good way to lay out the geography of a baseball diamond at all. Of course, the sun was then also directly into the catcher's eyes also. It was the same for both teams though, so it was something everyone had to deal with until the sun disappeared behind the school.

As luck would have it, in the bottom of the first inning, just as Roanoke sent their first player to the plate, Dimick started yelling, "Coach, I can't see!" Coach Siple came out of the dugout, called timeout, and walked to home plate. He asked Pete what the problem was, and Pete responded the sun was in his eyes and he couldn't see the pitched ball. Coach Siple asked, "You can't see the ball?" and Dimick replied, "No sir!" Coach Siple simply turned to the dugout and called out, "Mike Kenny, get your gear on." Mike was our back-up catcher, a good player and a really nice guy. Dimick was flabbergasted, and asked Coach why he was being taken out, and Coach Siple responded, "Well, if you can't see, you obviously can't play."

It was perfectly logical and made good sense, and "Redeye" trotted to the dugout with his head down. Of course, by the time Kenny got his catcher's gear on and made a few warm-up throws to second base, the setting sun was no longer a factor. It was about the sixth inning when Buddy Hobbs showed up. Buddy had hitchhiked all the way from Boys Home with his uniform on, to try and get to the game on time. I remember Coach barely looking at Buddy when he arrived, and he didn't put him into the game until the ninth inning. I grounded into a double play with a hard-hit ball to the shortstop late in the game. Damn slow legs Nunnally! We got beat by one run.

On the ride back after the game I amused myself by asking Dimick question after question about what he should have done. Like, "Redeye, why didn't you just call timeout, go out to the pitcher, and stall a little bit till the sun went down?" Or "Dimick, why didn't you tell the ump you broke the webbing on your catcher's mitt and go over to our dugout to get another mitt, and stall the time away?" Or, "Pete, why didn't you tell the ump you got dirt in your eye, and come over to the dugout to flush it out with water?"

Dimick was in the front seat with Coach Siple, and every time I'd ask him a question, he'd say, "Shut up Nunnally!" I'd look in the front mirror and see Coach Siple smiling, but he never said a word. I finally let up and Buddy, sitting next to me, spent the rest of the ride back to The Hill regaling us with his hitchhiking tales.

Unchained

22

SENIOR YEAR

September 1962 brought the start of my senior at Covington High School, and it proved to be a year full of challenges, accomplishments, and surprises. I was made a proctor in Greene Cottage and, along with Pete Dimick, was one of the leaders of Boys Home. We took advantage of our status as soon as school started, declaring that we were not going to switch tables in the dining hall. We stayed at Coach Siple's table the entire year!

I decided that if I got the opportunity, I was going to give college a try, but there still questions in my mind about how that was going to work. Were my grades good enough for me to get into college? Where would I go? Would I be playing sports? How would I pay for college if I wasn't good enough to get an athletic scholarship? Could I cut it and succeed in college? This was all stuff "normal" families dealt with, but I was clueless. I mentioned my concerns to Coach Siple and Chief, and they both said to just relax, these things would work themselves out during the year. I trusted them and tried to put my doubts out of my mind.

My friendship with Pete became even closer as we now shared the proctor's room and duties in Greene Cottage. Our job was to help Granny keep cottage life running smoothly, and to make sure the other thirteen boys were doing what they were supposed to. Mostly just focusing on stuff like keeping the cottage clean, making sure everyone was on time to meals and activities, reminding them to maintain proper decorum in study hall, and monitoring their behavior with each other.

It was usually easy, but there were times when we would have to break out a can of whip ass to get one or more of them back into line. And when I say "we," I mean Redeye most of the time. One thing that was never tolerated was sassing or giving Granny a hard time. That could get you in big trouble, and a severe talking to down in the basement. That hardly ever happened, as nearly everyone loved and respected her. A certain tradition of pride had been established in Greene, and most of the boys bought into it, making life easier on everybody.

That nine-by-fifteen proctor's room was tight living. Most of our time in the room together was in the evening, just before and after "lights out" for the cottage. Two single beds with a small space between them, and a single desk took up most of the room. We took turns using the desk when necessary, and while it never got dusty, it wasn't well worn from our use. There was a lot of bravado in that room, and not much talk of inner feelings. In a place like Boys Home, "feelings" showed weakness, and even though I loved that big red-headed dude, I seldom let my guard down around him or anyone else. Not until we cut the lights out at night did we ever share some of our doubts and fears; never to be brought up again between us in broad daylight.

We were hanging out in the basement one evening after study hall and I was talking about peroxiding my hair. Remember that when I came to The Hill, my nickname at that time had been Whitey, but as time passed, I went from there to blond to the now 'dirty blond.' I was ready for a change! It was a "town night" the next day, and I picked up a bottle of peroxide from the store, and the next afternoon I was getting ready to apply the whole bottle to my head, but I chickened out and just wet the bit in the front that hung down in my face if I didn't comb it. I was sitting in the sun until it dried, then went inside and looked in the mirror. I liked it! Then went outside and wet a little more. I liked that result too and continued to peroxide my hair for many years after. As I sit typing this, I could again be called Whitey—without any additions of peroxide to my hair.

I guess Dimick couldn't stand feeling left out though; the next night in the basement he came down with some shaving cream and a razor. He said, "I'm going to shave my head! A few years later when in *Cool Hand Luke*, Paul Newman declared, "I can eat fifty eggs," that reminded me so much of Redeye. Just so random and out of the blue!

That wasn't the end of the shaving though. Another evening after school had been in session for a while, we were in the basement hanging out and smoking, playing a harmless game of who could take the hardest hit on the arm without howling. This kind of stuff passed for fun back in the day! Guys would take turns just blasting another guy in the upper part of their arm, to see who could take it. I declared early on that as a proctor, I was exempt, and besides I needed both my arms for basketball and baseball. I was just a wee bit smarter than most.

Dimick came down with the shaving cream and razor to steal the show. He was dating a girl named Donna and decided to shave a big "D" on his chest! He was a big boy with red hair, and he had red hair all over his body! The normal places guys have hair, plus his back, the tops of his arms, everywhere! His chest hair looked thick like a blanket and was at least and inch and a half long. He got someone to help with this shaving, he wanted it perfect! A few minutes later, there it was, the "D"—representing both Donna and DDD—Donald Darwin Dimick! Kind of a drag when they broke up though.

That year, the football team was dominating, and before I knew it, it was time for Homecoming. I wasn't dating anyone steady at the time, and evidently neither was Marie Smith. I was happy to be her escort to the Homecoming Game, and lo and behold, she was crowned Queen by a vote of the student body. Those were the good old days, so no room for a Homecoming King. The Cougars beat William Byrd to push their record to 8-0. I had a great time at the Homecoming Dance, and there were lots of slow songs that filled the air! The following Friday night the Cougars were defeated by William Fleming of Roanoke 7-6, thus ending their chance of an undefeated season. They bounced back the next week however, trouncing our archrival Clifton Forge 47-14, as coach Boodie Albert finally gave Dimick his wish and let him play running back. He was a terror, looking for tacklers to hit!

We all got a special treat that fall, as Chief Burrowes had somehow made provisions for everyone on The Hill to travel to Roanoke for the Harvest Bowl football game between VPI and UVA. We piled in our buses and drove the sixty or so miles to Roanoke, excited to see not only the football game, but also the big parade beforehand. The game was played at Victory Stadium, which had a seating capacity of twenty-five thousand. The stands were packed for this in-state rivalry, and VPI prevailed 20-15. I got to see Tommy Walker run the ball for the "Hokies" and I went down on the field to see him after the game. He introduced me to some of his teammates, and to his coach Jerry Claiborne. All the other boys were asking me how it felt to be on the field, and I couldn't lie, it was exciting!

After the game we went to the posh Hotel Roanoke for a catered dinner, and Chief was beaming with pride at the way his boys looked and conducted themselves while being introduced to what I guess were the donors who made the trip possible. There was lots of early excitement on the buses talking about the day, and then lots of sleep on the way home.

23

BEGGING FOR MONEY

One of the main jobs Bob Burrowes had was raising money to support the program at Boys Home. Now, Chief was an intelligent, outgoing man who was a dapper dresser, and fundraising was right up his alley. The following is taken from the History section of the Boys Home website (www.boyshomeinc.com).

> Robert F. Burrowes became director in 1946, and he oversaw the completion of the first modern cottage and a building program that lasted over 20 years.
> With help from Col. Parry W. Lewis, Bob Burrowes started a comprehensive fundraising system so that future construction wouldn't incur large indebtedness.

The best way to get people excited enough to financially support something like Boys Home is to get face time with them. And of course, it doesn't hurt to have some exhibits to show them either. Chief understood this tug on the heart strings well. Whose heart wouldn't melt when a couple of clean-cut young boys were presented as examples of the good work that went on up at The Hill? When Dimick and I became seniors, Chief began to take us with him to help put a face on the Boys Home story and mission. We jokingly called it begging for money!

There were no overnight trips, but I remember logging some long hours in the Home station wagon. Typically, these trips would be on weekends, and often we would be taken to Episcopal churches on Sundays. I also remember several trips to civic-minded organizations, such as the Rotary Club.

These trips and conversations with Chief Burrowes gave me an insight into the outside world that I would not otherwise have had. We were good ambassadors for the Home, and could work the crowd, looking and acting like the puppy dog you just have to take home—without the licking of course!

We learned how to stand relaxed but upright, look people in the eye as they asked us questions, and to avoid feeding our faces too much when the inevitable spread was put on the table. Being Home Boys however, we couldn't resist stuffing our pockets with goodies when the crowd thinned out and wasn't focused on us. The best part about being "orphans" and " begging for money" was the extra special clothes we were allowed to buy. Chief understood the importance of a good appearance, and so he made sure we were stylish on these trips.

Ordinarily we did our shopping at Leggett in Covington, or brought clothes back with us after vacations that were purchased by parents/foster parents/guardians. Leggett was your very basic department store and they were a successful chain for several years. Decent clothes, not very stylish, OK quality. At the beginning of our senior year however, Chief personally took Pete and me to Rooklin's to shop! Now Rooklin's was what passed for preppy clothes in Covington in those days.

Of course, Pete and I were like kids in a candy store, wanting this and wanting that. Chief brought us down to reality quickly, however, and he helped us pick out a couple of complete outfits to wear on the road. He also used that time to explain to us the importance of "dressing for success," although he didn't use those exact words. Granny praised us up and down when she saw us in our new finery.

This experience of "begging for money," along with other things like hitchhiking, playing sports, etc., combined with my own personality and natural tendencies, has allowed me to learn to be comfortable in my own skin. I can pretty much hang with anybody or any group and feel comfortable. However, I have also learned through the years that I need to get out of my comfort zone and stretch myself in order to expand my world.

When we came out of Rooklin's with our clothes, Chief looked askance at my peroxided hair, but told Dimick he couldn't go begging for money until his hair grew out! That gave me some special time alone with Mr. Burrowes for a month or so. We talked about my future, and he let me know he had high hopes for me, both in college and beyond. Chief never gave up on me, even when I let him, myself, and others down.

I remember it was before basketball season had started when my friend and fellow senior, Randy Powell, started talking to me about singing in a band. I told him to get serious, and he said he was. Randy was one of the nicest guys you could ever meet, and he had a unique story. Randy had grown up in Covington, on Fudge Street, with his mom and dad. I'm not totally clear on what happened, but his dad was out of the picture, and Mrs. Powell, his mom, came up on The Hill to be a housemother. Randy came with her and lived as a Home Boy in her cottage, Darling or Whitehead. I believe this happened his sophomore or junior year at CHS. He had been the team manager for the Varsity Basketball team the previous year, and my junior year he was going to be on the team as a sub.

I knew Randy played the guitar, but it turns out he was a serious musician, quite unlike me, who liked singing for attention! After school one day, he and I headed across the street from the high school to the local radio station, where I met one of the local DJs, Les King. I guess Les was in his forties, and he was a keyboard player. Also with us was Stanley Walker, a junior at CHS. Stanley played the drums. We played together a little bit in the station studio and "The Searchers" became a reality! I couldn't believe it. All that singing had finally paid off.

After that, we started having serious practice sessions, working on popular covers and establishing a core group of songs from which to form a playlist, which changed from gig to gig, depending on the audience. I remember *The Twist, Tossin' and Turnin', Travelin' Man, Cathy's Clown, A Teenager in Love,* and of course a couple by Elvis. It was harder than I thought it would be, but eventually Les said it was time to hit the airways. On a Saturday morning, live from the WKEY Covington studios, we made our debut. Soon after, we were booked for our first paying gig, a sock hop at the Armory next door to the studio.

I wasn't that nervous, as I knew most of the kids who attended, and they had heard me sing plenty of times before. Throw in some seventh and eighth graders, and it was a successful first time out. We didn't practice much after that, as basketball season was soon upon us, and Randy and I didn't have much free time. We didn't play a lot of dances, but enough to earn some cash that Chief Burrowes made sure I put away for college.

I learned about Mother Vineyard Wine from Stanley during band breaks, and that was my first real introduction to alcohol. The biggest gig I remember we had was playing at the Greenbrier, a big resort in White Sulphur Springs, West Virginia. We played for the annual DC Transit party, which changed their name to Metro in 1976. The Greenbrier was, and still is, quite the resort.

One thing that stood out to me that night was how much I made per song. I figured I made twenty-five dollars per song. A fortune to me in those days. Our set was cut short to allow time for a professional dance couple to teach the crowd how to dance the bossa nova, a blend of samba and jazz that came from Brazil. (There was a popular song: *Blame it on the Bossa Nova.*)

By the time they had finished their dance lessons, we had time for only a couple more songs. It was a great evening though.

Alas, my singing career got cut short in the spring by a business decision. Les hired a guy to take my place who could sing *and* play lead guitar. I really didn't mind; it was near the end of my time on The Hill and I was already "goodbye" in my mind.

Unchained

24

LAST SEASONS

Coming off of a 14-3 season with only one starter to replace, we knew we could have a special hoops season, and we did. Our area had some good athletes in those days, but no basketball team could compare to ours. Of our top three players, Dimick was a scholarship football player, Buddy Hobbs signed a pro baseball contract upon graduation, and peroxided Nunnally played basketball and baseball for Bridgewater College. Our remaining two, Pete Davis and Bobby Davidson, could play for anybody around. Of course, we knew all the players on the Cougar hoops squad, we had grown up with them in school, and played against them in P.E. We begged coach Siple to schedule a game with them, but he said their schedule wouldn't allow it.

Damn it! They had a player I was dying to play against! Butch Paxton was their leading scorer, but I had seen him play and I thought he was what we called "a gunner." That meant he took a lot of shots, so naturally he would score. They ended the season 6-12, and yeah, I still believe it would have been 6-13 had we played them!

I had been spending a lot of time in the gym, working on my game. My hook shot had gotten deadly from twelve feet in, and it was my "go to" when I faced taller players. When I practiced by myself, which I often did, I was Zeke from Cabin Creek, Jerry West. He played shooting guard for West Virginia, and later played for the Los Angeles Lakers. I never lost a game as

Zeke, for we were always down one point when I took that last shot with time running out. If I made it, we won; if I missed, I was fouled. Then two foul shots to score the win. What if I missed either of them? The opponents were in the lane too soon on the foul shot, so I got another. I always walked off the solo court a winner.

And that's just the way it was when we played the Bridgewater College JV team again. We were undefeated just as we had been the previous season when we played them. We knew we had our work cut out for us. We hung tight with them, and at halftime Coach said keep it close and we would win at the end. I took a hard foul that wasn't called and lost my temper, got a technical, and lost my focus for a couple of minutes. That was enough to put us behind by three, and we never caught up. This year though, we powered through our last couple of games, and finished the season 17-1. This is still the best winning percentage held by any Hilltopper team, and that sign is still on the wall just outside the entrance to the gym!

Spring was in the air at CHS, and, as seniors, we could see the end in sight. I had taken the SATs for college entrance and done so-so and had filled out my application to Bridgewater College. I had also looked at Hampden-Sydney, but once I learned it was an all-male school, I ruled that out immediately. Coach Siple felt I would get into Bridgewater. He reminded me that he had scheduled them in basketball the past two years so their coach would get to see me play. He also said I would be good enough to play baseball there if I wanted to.

All the college-bound kids were talking about where they were headed in the fall, and I was happy to be able to join in when Bridgewater sent me my acceptance letter. Redeye didn't know yet where he was headed, but he didn't seem too terribly worried about it. He had just gotten word that he had been selected an Honorable-Mention All-American football player, and was waiting to see what scholarship offers would be coming in.

With all but one returning starter, the Hilltopper baseball team was again undefeated, with Junior Buddy Hobbs leading the way on the mound. After the season, Coach Siple, who was then what was called a "bird-dog scout" with the Pittsburg Pirates, took Dimick and me to a couple of tryout camps for professional baseball players. I wasn't thinking in that direction, but I was curious and agree to go. A road trip and free food, right up a Home Boy's alley. Coach took Dimick and me, and another local player to tryout camps in both Salem and Richmond. There were a lot of guys at each camp, and naturally they were all pretty good. Position players, outfielders, infielders, etc., were put through our paces defensively, and then the pitchers and hitters went at it.

At the first camp in Salem, I soon realized this was a big step up in competition. Although my fastball had plenty of zip on it, I wasn't overpowering the hitters like I was used to. I got roughed up at first, then settled in and spotted my pitches better. It became evident however, that my curveball was lacking. All in all, I felt that I was about middle of the road with the group. Dimick did OK too, but he didn't stand out among the catchers either. The second tryout camp in Richmond didn't go that well for me. It was pretty much "throw it and duck"! That means I was ducking from all of the line-drives coming back at me. A lot of the guys in this camp were older, and some had even played some minor league ball. I wasn't too discouraged however, as I didn't really have any aspirations to play professional baseball. I knew I wasn't of that caliber. If there was any doubt about that however, it was dispelled by the man who was running the tryout camps for the Pirates. His name was Syd Thrift, and he knew coach Siple well.

At the conclusion of the camp, he put his arm around me and said something like, "Nunnally, you've got a pretty good fifty-eight-foot fastball, but I suggest you plan on going to college. Now the distance from the pitcher's mound to home plate is sixty feet and six inches. This was his way of telling me I didn't throw hard enough to be a professional baseball player.

Syd Thrift surely knew how to evaluate talent, as he spent fifty years in baseball with several different teams and was general manager of the Pirates from '85–'88. He was out of baseball for a number of years before that, and had a successful real estate business in Fairfax, Virginia. But he still did some work at local baseball clinics. I was coaching at Park View H.S. in Sterling, (Loudoun County, right next to Fairfax), and attended one of the clinics where he was the headliner. After his presentation, I went up and introduced myself, and asked him if he remembered me. Syd laughed and said, "Hell, no. Why would I?"

I had started ironing my clothes when I moved to Greene Cottage from Jack Gordon. The high school boys on The Hill took a lot of pride in their appearance, and that was passed down to me from the older boys in the cottage. Plus, you had to look good if you wanted to land a girlfriend. There was a weekly commercial laundry service for us, but our clothes always came back like they had folded them into a square, and then pressed with a very hot two-thousand pound flat metal beam. They would be squished flat with wrinkles so sharp you couldn't iron them out. I can't remember who, but some older boy taught me to iron both shirts and pants.

I was downstairs in the kitchen getting ready to iron a shirt to wear the last week of school. The bus would be there to take us to school in fifteen minutes or so, and I had put off ironing my shirt till the last minute. Most of the boys in the cottage were already either at the bus stop or on their way.

Just as the iron got hot, Pete came bounding down the stairs with his big hairy chest showing and a shirt in his hand. He demanded that I hand the iron over to him so he could iron his shirt. I basically said no dice, I was here first, and he could iron his shirt when I got finished. Pete said in that husky, gravelly voice of his, "Nunnally, give me that iron!" I again said no, he could wait until I was finished. He said, "If you don't give me that iron, I'm going to take it away from you!"

Now Pete and I were like real brothers at this point, and I couldn't believe he was trying to pull the "I can kick your butt if I want to" card. He was the big dog on the porch at Boys Home, there was no doubt about it. He now stood about six-foot-one, and probably weighed between 220 and 230 pounds. He sported lots of muscle due to consistent weightlifting down in the cottage basement. Usually when he wanted something it was like that scene in the Ten Commandments when Pharaoh gave an order: "So let it be written; so let it be done." Now, at this time, I stood six-foot-three, and weighed 175, wringing wet. But I just couldn't believe he was trying to order me around.

We didn't have that kind of relationship, and besides, Dimick, as big as he was, was not a bully. When he got something in his head, however, that was the way it was going to be. Just as I was shaking my head "No!," he took me out with one swing.

Pete hit me with a right hook and boom, I was out like a light! When I woke up a few seconds later, Dimick was kneeling down beside me with silent tears in his eyes. He pulled me to my feet and could not stop apologizing for hitting me. It was the first and only time he ever laid a hand on me in anger. I was rubbing my jaw, still dazed, and Pete said, "Here, I'll iron your shirt for you." When he finished mine, I put it on and waited for him to finish ironing his. As we were on our way to the bus, Pete kept saying, I'm sorry Nunnally, I was just stupid."

For the next couple of weeks, he felt so guilty he was all about doing anything I wanted him to. Of course, I took advantage of those opportunities. Hell, I was just glad Pete didn't break my jaw. My son Pete is named after the man/boy that I shared so much of my life on The Hill with. Donald Darwin Dimick was certainly one of a kind.

One of my favorite classes at CHS was government, which all students took in their senior year. It was interesting to learn how our government worked, and I really enjoyed the teacher, Gay Parker. She was on the younger side, had a lot of spunk, and seemed to really enjoy her job. Pete sat behind me in her class, and felt the same way about Ms. Parker. We sat next to these big, long windows, that would be opened in the days before air conditioning, and Pete and I cooked up a way to have a little fun. Ms. Parker spent a lot of time at the chalkboard diagramming the different parts and responsibilities of the three branches of government. One day as she had her back to the class, Dimick and I hopped out of the window to the ground about five feet below, and then ran back into the school. Imagine the surprise on Gay Parker's face when she opened the classroom door after hearing the knocking. The second time we pulled that stunt was the last however, as she wasn't smiling as we made our way back to our desks!

The big day was here! Graduation! Etta Walker was there with Joyce Fay, and my sister Celia was in attendance with Herb and their young son, Todd. It was anticlimactic for me in a way, as all my classmates were having parties, etc., and I was back on The Hill by nine. I hadn't been invited to any celebrations, which was a bit of a downer. Aside from my brothers on The Hill, and Temple Kessinger, I really didn't have any good friends. I had some friendly acquaintances at CHS, but I really didn't have the time or opportunity outside of school to foster any meaningful relationships with my peers in Covington. I had no car, joined no clubs because of transportation issues, and of course played basketball and baseball for the Hilltoppers. I was basically a "loner," as is evidenced by my senior yearbook, the only one I bought while in high school. Under my senior picture, where they normally listed all of the sports and other activities a student had participated in during his or her four years in high school, was a big ole blank spot! All my activities were on The Hill and didn't count at CHS.

Whereas lots of kids would write in each other's yearbooks, especially their senior book, there is one short entry from a gal I dated very briefly. The day everyone received their yearbook she saw me in the hall on the way to the bus home and asked me to write in her book. I couldn't say no, so I scribbled something and handed her my yearbook when she asked. I never brought it back to school for any signing opportunities. I felt it was superficial, and I wasn't really interested in just making up some nonsense like, "Stay cool!" "Remember all the good times," "You're a really nice girl" etc. That was just not my style.

My seven years as a Boys Home resident would be over in a couple of days, and although I didn't really reflect on those years at that time, here is what I know now: Boys Home saved my life! Had I continued living with my mother and stepfather in Norfolk I would have eventually followed the path of a hoodlum, a criminal, or, as the psychiatrist stated in my evaluation, developed a mental disease. That pathway would have led to some dark places, with some dark outcomes.

Life on The Hill gave me the structure and foundation to enable me to have a chance, an opportunity for a life I could be proud of. A life grounded in a value system of fundamental truths, of faith, of brotherhood, sympathy, the golden rule, and many more positive attributes that would guide me toward a life of service to others.

The firm yet loving guidance and examples set forth by the staff, especially Granny Myers, Chief Burrowes, and Coach Siple helped shape and mold an emotionally mixed-up kid into someone who could see possibilities of a life well lived. There were no earth-shattering events that influenced me, but rather the steady drumbeat of doing the right thing the right way that eventually imbedded itself into my psyche. I had a blueprint.

Unchained

INTERLUDE

These words from a Staff Manual for Boys Home in 1971 sum up the basic Philosophy and Purpose of Boys Home (which was still "Boys' Home" at that date).

Boys' Home was established to provide care for boys who either had no suitable home or who had problems which might best be solved by placement away from their homes. Over the years with the growing complexities of society, the problems of assisting these children to grow into well adjusted adults have also increased.

Caring for these youngsters entrusted to us entails a great deal. We, at Boys' Home, are directly responsible not only for the provision of food, clothing, and shelter, but are also entrusted with the tremendous responsibility of molding the character of these boys. During these formative years, habits and traits are established which will largely determine success or failure in later life.

To instill basic principles of honesty, loyalty, courtesy, love, kindness, religion, and education into each child must be our ultimate goal. Achieving this requires the utmost effort on the part of each staff member working in cooperation with his fellow workers.

. . . The raw material with which we work is very sensitive. Who knows when you may be chosen as the "hero" of some lad or the person he most admires. Each staff member's life must be so conducted as to set a good example for the children. It is no easy job and all will fail at some time, for we are only human . . . The staff member must be a well adjusted, matured individual with kindness, patience, understanding, and—above all—a love of his fellow creatures. He must realize that each child is an individual and each must be dealt with as an individual. Each child at Boys' Home has had difficulties of some nature with adults and adult standards. Many are suspicious and distrustful. It is up to the staff to exhibit fairness and justice, to act firmly when firmness is required, but to hear the child's side of the story, before acting.

As I read through the above words from the '71 staff manual again, I can't help but reflect on those staff who I have mentioned who met those goals on my behalf. Wouldn't it be wonderful if every parent of every child who is brought into the world was presented with those words of purpose and mission?

As I departed Boys Home, I had a blueprint, but not a roadmap.

It was like this for me; Imagine a young colt in a Western movie, who had been nurtured and trained in a small circular corral. One day the gate is flung open, and the colt is set free to roam at will. The colt rushes out into the fresh grass, nostrils flaring with excitement, mane and tail flowing behind with the rush of the wind caused by his flashing hooves on the ground. It can be made into a beautiful cinematic, feel-good moment. But what isn't shown in the movie is what the colt does when the adrenaline rush is over, the colt gets tired and hungry, and then doesn't know where to head or what to do next.

The structure and cocoon I had been living in for seven years had saved me, but I wasn't self-disciplined enough to follow that blueprint on my own. So, I floundered and paid the price for that in different ways. It was tough because I didn't have anyone or anyplace to fall back on. No one to call for advice, for support, or a shoulder to lean on. I was out there on my own, trying to figure out for the first time who Mike Nunnally really was. I had a lot of self-confidence, was headstrong, had a "devil may care" attitude, with that roguish grin the psychiatrist mentioned in his report some seven years earlier. My emotional health was not good, however. All the baggage I carried with me to Boys Home as the result of my abuse was still there. I had gotten better at hiding it, and in some cases dealing with it, but it was going to be a long slog before I finally came to grips with the events in my life in Norfolk, Virginia.

Unchained

25

SUMMER JOBS

After graduation, Dimick and I had each rented a room in the same boarding house in town and were trying to earn some spending money for our freshman year of college in the fall. I had known for a while that I was going to Bridgewater College in the Shenandoah Valley of Virginia, and "Redeye" had decided to go to the Midwest to play football for Northeastern Oklahoma A & M Junior College. (That team played in the Junior Rose Bowl his freshman season).

I forget what Dimick was doing for that minimum wage of $1.25 per hour, but he had the better of the jobs, no doubt.

My first job was working west of Covington for a company that was laying huge concrete pipes along some roadway. I would get picked up in Covington at six-thirty a.m., we would start work at seven and knock off at five-thirty p.m., with a half hour for (unpaid) lunch. Six days a week, ten hours a day! The only good thing about the job was that we would get time and a half for the twenty hours we worked past the normal forty-hour week. This meant I was making $88.50 per week.

Rent and food were cheap, and I was usually too tired to do anything but work, so I figured to bank a lot of money that summer. The work was very physical, and most days it got really hot. Once the pipe was laid, this guy on a bulldozer would push the dirt up next to it and my job was to shovel it closer to the pipe and then tamp it down. They had these gas-operated machines, like jackhammers except they had a flat square head on the business end. I came to hate those things. At the end of the workday, it would take at least an hour for my skinny body to stop shaking.

Working with the other guys was quite an education though. I was the only "college boy" on the job, and the other guys kept me smiling and laughing with their mostly good-natured banter. I got friendly with the bulldozer operator and was amazed when he told me he was paid twenty dollars per hour!

The company provided water for us to drink during the day, and I'm not sure where they got it, but after four backbreaking weeks on the job I got dysentery. I missed three straight days of work, and when I tried to get on the truck the next day, the driver told me I had been replaced, that they couldn't wait for me to get well. I've got to tell you; I was not disappointed. I figured I could get another job quickly.

I talked to Dimick and he said he knew a man who was looking for some guys who were skilled at manual labor. That was me all right! I went to see his friend and the next day began my work with a company that was building bridges for Interstate 64 that was just being constructed. This job wasn't as physically demanding as the pipeline gig, but it got a bit hairy walking on the steel spikes, especially early in the morning when the dew was still prevalent. The pay was the same, but it was an eight-hour day, Monday through Friday. After three weeks or so on this job, I knew the summer would soon be coming to an end, and I would be off to a new life as a freshman in college.

The bridge required a lot of concrete, and typically concrete requires reinforcing bar (rebar) to help bind it and keep it from cracking. Rebar is usually made of steel, and was delivered and installed by a company and crew totally separate from the one I worked for. The rebar was woven through these metal spikes that top the steel beams of the bridge, and then the concrete was poured. Wooden forms constructed by carpenters gave the concrete its shape.

One morning the rebar guys show up, but they are short one crew member. My boss tells me to fill in for him, and I start teaming up with two other guys to carry these long, flexible bars of steel. We carried a few of them at a time, and it was hard work. The rebar crew had special pads for their shoulders, but I rigged my T-shirt as best I could. Still it wasn't long before my shoulder was rubbed raw, and I was hurting. I held my own, and thankfully it was soon time for lunch.

While we were eating someone asked the rebar crew what they made, and they said $1.75 per hour. My ears perked up, and I thought to myself, if they were getting that much, I should too, since I was doing the same work. I went to my foreman and explained the situation and told him I felt it was fair that my hourly rate would be $1.75 while I was working with the rebar crew, including the four hours I had already put in that morning. He essentially said no way that was going to happen, and that I should get ready to start carrying rebar in five minutes. I asked him again to see the logic in my request, and he basically blew me off. "Because I said so." That attitude has always stuck in my craw. The bridge foreman didn't use those exact words, but that's what I heard.

It was logical to me that I should receive the same pay as the other rebar laborers, but my boss didn't want to change the status quo. I walked up to him, shook his hand, and said it had been nice working for him, but I was quitting.

So, I walked off the job after lunch. It was my second job of the summer.

I have always been willing to stand up and speak up for what I believe in. I'm not one to shut my mouth and meekly follow along when I am confronted with a situation that doesn't feel right to me. Many times, I knew that the outcome wasn't going to be changed by what I said or did, or by the stance I took, but that didn't matter to me. "To thine own self be true." Over the course of my life, I have paid the price for that part of my make-up, and there have obviously been times when I was wrongheaded, but that's just part of me being a Boys Home Boy. I had learned that being true to self was the best way for me to be, not just depending on situational ethics to guide me.

SECTION THREE
COLLEGE—ARMY—COLLEGE

Unchained

26

IN MY ROOM

Bridgewater College was founded in 1880 and was the first four-year liberal arts college in Virginia to admit both men and women. Turns out, in the fall of '63, there were only about 655 students on campus, near the same number of students at CHS. I hadn't done a lot of research on the college and had no idea it was that small! Nestled in the beautiful Shenandoah Valley of Virginia, about eight miles from Harrisonburg, Bridgewater was associated with the Church of the Brethren, once known as the "Dunkers." The Dunkers baptized with total submersion and espouse no creed. The Brethren emphasize peace, simplicity, the equality of believers, and consistent obedience to Christ.

Bridgewater had a mandatory chapel once a week, and believe it or not, they took attendance. I went to the first few but was soon looking for a way out. Chapel wasn't a religious service, and no hymns were sung that I can remember, just someone giving a talk on one subject or another. I found out one of my female friends was someone who took attendance, and she cut me a break.

I lived my freshman year in Wardo Hall, a dilapidated all-male dorm that was at one end of the campus. It was a rowdy place, with a bunch of freshman guys who got along well. The college issued all incoming Freshman a crimson and gold beanie that we were supposed to wear anytime we were out and about on the campus. A form of initiation that was to last until the Homecoming football game. A bunch of us who lived in Wardo thought the idea was way too hokey and we refused to wear it. Turns out it wasn't that important, as no one who had any authority took us to task for that violation. There were a couple of other rules that the students thought were onerous that were challenged in the spring.

I was taking the general studies classes that all Freshman were required to take their first year before declaring a major, and I quickly fell into a routine of putting off any assignments until the last minute. With no mandatory study hall like we had on The Hill, I did not learn to put a plan in place until it was too late.

I easily made friends, and dorm living was a trouble-free adjustment for me as this was what I had been used to for the past seven years. How was I able to quickly make friends when I had very few while at CHS? I guess it was because I felt I was on equal footing with my classmates at Bridgewater. No one knew my story, or that I had lived in a home for boys. A very few of my college friends would learn some of that later, but nothing in real depth.

It was a new beginning for me, in a whole new world. As soon as I could, I made my way to that cozy gym to play pick-up basketball, mostly with guys I was hoping to be playing with during the upcoming season. There were several good players out there, and as I played against them, my game naturally started getting better. These guys played hard! The Varsity basketball coach, Melvin "Shifty" Myers, had his offices in the complex, and would poke his head in from time to time to watch the action. I had met him late in the spring before graduation, and after we exchanged pleasantries in the gym, he said he was glad I had chosen to attend Bridgewater, and that he looked forward to working with me.

That short conversation got me very excited, because it gave me hope I could possibility make the Varsity Eagle squad this season. I mean honestly, basketball and baseball were the only reason I had decided to attend college at all. That's maybe not a good reason for some to hear, but it's the truth. At any rate, it was a big step forward for this boy.

Although I kept my life prior to living at Boys Home to myself, all the emotional baggage I had acquired was still there, and it continued to flare up from time to time. I have always loved music, and the Beach Boys released a song in '63 that really spoke to me. I sang it constantly to myself. It was called *In My Room*, and spoke of a make-believe place where I could go, close the door, and escape from my worries and fears. There I could dream big dreams, pray them into being, and if they didn't pan out, I could either laugh or cry about it. I found a lot of comfort repeating those lyrics.

The structure, program, and staff at Boys Home had kept me from acting out, but once I left that environment, I had trouble controlling my emotions, and could fill with anger quickly and blow up, either verbally or physically. The first time I met Betty Kline was one such case. I got in an argument with a male student in the gym over a basketball game, and had put my hand through a window in frustration. Betty was a psychology professor, and someone asked her to talk with me. I was in the gym when she found me crying in frustration. It was the first of many conversations we had when I was a student, as the next year Betty became the Assistant Dean of Students.

Betty had graduated from Bridgewater in 1955, so she was young in my eyes. She had a very calm voice, was a good listener, and was not judgmental. She was the first person I ever told the whole story of my childhood. It was such a relief to me to be able to spill my guts to someone I trusted. Betty and her husband, Paul, who was the art professor at Bridgewater, became very good friends of mine over the years. Spending time with them and their three children showed me how a loving family was possible, and they became my role models in parenthood and in many other ways!

I was on a work-study program until basketball tryouts to help offset some of my tuition costs, and so I volunteered to work in the dish room at the central dining hall, where all of the students took their meals. I worked the same job that I had taken at Boys Home to make a little extra money, using a hose to prewash the dishes before they went into the automated dishwasher. The students were supposed to bring their tray full of dishes to the small, narrow opening, scrape their plates of any leftover food, then stack the dishes and trays, and put the cutlery in a water bin to soak. My job was to give the scraped dishes a quick rinse and then pass them down to get put into the dish rack for washing.

People being people, there are always going to be some who don't follow the proper protocol, and so I found that some students weren't bothering to scrape their food off the dishes properly. They would just basically shove them in and walk away. Hollering at them, who were mostly guys, didn't seem to have an effect, and I couldn't really see who it was because of the way the food drop off was set up, but I could see their backside as they walked away. Now the hose I was using had a strong stream, and I found it could shoot water several feet into the air. It didn't take me long to train those folks to scrape those dishes properly. Wet butt is not a good look! Of course, a couple of the guys kind of threatened me, but I just laughed at them. Boys Home Boy!

Bridgewater was a "dry" campus, no alcohol allowed. In addition, freshmen were not allowed to have a car on campus, which didn't bother me as I had no car, and no driver's license. I wouldn't own my own car until 1970. Classes were held six days a week, including Saturdays, and except for labs, all classes were over by noon. With all these factors coming into play, my social life was confined to campus.

I did, however, have my eye on a fellow freshman athlete named Pat Kloes, and we started hanging out together. Pat was thin, about five-foot-ten, and quite the basketball player. In fact, Pat Nunnally is listed as the second leading all-time scorer in Bridgewater women's basketball history. Pat was cute, smart, and a lot of fun to be around. We started getting serious about the time basketball tryouts started and were in the foyer of the gym one afternoon kissing goodbye when coach Myers came around the corner. We didn't see him as he blew his whistle and yelled, "Jump Ball"! We all got a good laugh out of that!

It turns out I was doing what a lot of Home Boys have done; grabbed at the first person I thought could love me. I guess I was desperate for someone to belong to, and Pat was my lifeline at that point. It was fabulous! I was head over heels in love!

Basketball tryouts were tough, and I realized that if I made the Varsity squad, I would be spending a lot of time on the" pines" (the bench). That didn't really bother me, I loved basketball and liked every one of the other players. I was ready to get better and wait my turn. Just before our first pre-season scrimmage, they took a team picture, and there I am in the 1964 yearbook standing tall and proud in my Varsity uniform!

The team went to Charlottesville for a preseason scrimmage against the UVA freshman team. Now we had freshman through seniors on our team, but it was still a very competitive scrimmage, as UVA's freshman team had a bunch of scholarship players on the squad.

In those days freshmen were not allowed to play on the Varsity squad at D1 (division 1) schools. A lot of people don't understand that the skill sets of D1 and D3 are not that far apart. In fact, many D3 players are more fundamentally sound that their D1 counterparts. The big difference in performance comes down to size, speed, and strength, with the D1 athlete usually holding an obvious edge there. So the scrimmage started, but I didn't. No surprise there. I did get a fair amount of playing time though and had what I thought was a pretty good outing. In the locker room after the scrimmage, I was checking with the stat guy to see how many rebounds I had gotten, as I prided myself on that aspect of the game. I relished being able to "block out" and rebound against bigger players.

Now Coach Myers, like many coaches (me included) was a very emotional guy, and he wasn't too happy with the way we had played as a team. He saw me looking at the stat sheet and said something like "Nunnally, what are you doing, trying to see how many points you got?"

You might say I got a bit peeved at that accusation, for I have always been a team player, and have never thirsted for individual acclaim or accomplishments. I hollered right back at Coach Myers, and said I was checking to see how many rebounds I got.

I "probably" followed that up with some other statements that made Coach Myers mad, and then he said that I was not going to be on the Varsity team, but would spend the year on the freshman team. Two emotional guys, in the heat of the moment, saying things they would both later regret. Of course, it was my fault. I should have kept my big mouth shut. But again, not my strong suit. I did enjoy my season on the freshman team, however. I got to start and play most of the game, and I got to hone my leadership skills, and to really begin the process that led me into coaching.

The freshman coach was a nice guy and gave it his all, but I don't think basketball was his specialty. As a result, we players had a little more say in what strategy and other aspects of the game that we employed. For example, we got blown out by Staunton Military Academy 99-66 at their place. There was no way we could compete with the talent they had. At practice the day before we were to play them at our place, I suggested that we play a slowdown game against them, to give ourselves a chance to win. This was before the shot clock came into being for basketball. The coach agreed to try it, and the next day we led 17-14 at halftime!

We ended up losing 33-31, but we were competitive and gave those boys quite a scare. I think I missed a shot at the end of the game that would have tied it up, but we were all satisfied with our effort. That game showed me that I had leadership abilities, that people would follow me if I tried to rally them around a positive common cause!

The highlight of the year for me was when we played Augusta Military Academy at home. I had four points at the half, in a close game. The guy who was guarding me started talking smack at the beginning of the second half, and I hit a couple of shots right away. The stands began to fill up with students who were coming to see the Varsity game, and they got into it and were encouraging me. My teammates started feeding me and I put up thirty-three points total in those twenty minutes. We won going away, but more importantly, the fans yelling and getting behind me for the first time made me feel like I was a part of "us"! Up until that point, I had been on campus for three or four months but had not really felt I was accepted, or part of the community. That night was a turning point for me in that regard.

Christmas break, exams, and the end of basketball came quickly. Despite my lack of effort in my studies, I did remain athletically eligible at the end of the first semester—barely. I was required to maintain a 1.8 GPA, and I barely made it. Flunking Spanish didn't help.

Unchained

27

SPRING IS IN THE AIR

Baseball was up next, and I was competing for the number one pitcher's spot. I had never seen the baseball team play, but I knew a bunch of the guys by then. A fellow freshman, Ray Heatwole, had played basketball with me, and I liked him a lot.

As it turns out, Ray became a very successful baseball coach at nearby Turner Ashby High School, and coached at James Madison University (JMU) for a few years. We bumped into each other over the years when I was coaching at Park View High School, as our teams competed against one another in baseball. His teams got the best of us several times, but in 1984 we bested them on the way to a State Championship!

Most of the guys on the baseball team also played either football or basketball, as was the case with a lot of other small colleges in those days. It was a good bunch to hang and play with, and I was accepted immediately. Three of the veterans, Lee Dellinger, Yager Marks, and Delmar Bodkin, took me under their wing and settled me down when my emotions got the better of me. We had fun and had a winning season. I don't know who did the scheduling, but the little ole Eagles played Bucknell, West Virginia, University of Maine, and Catholic University. That's a heavy lift!

I had a good year on the mound, but we got beat by West Virginia 5-1 after I ran out of gas in the sixth inning. I was so pumped up my arm hurt for a week after throwing as hard as I could in the blowing snow. I got along with the coach, but I didn't care for his style. One example: We took a couple of vans to play a double header at Old Dominion. We slept at their place in a big room with double bunk beds. Coach gave a curfew for us as we wanted to hit the town of Norfolk for a bit and warned us of consequences if we were late. The group I was with was back on time, but the other van missed the time by about thirty minutes. I was awake when they came in, and watched as the coach pretended to be asleep, but peeked out under his hand to watch the players come in. Nothing was ever mentioned about them being late. Lame sauce. He was no coach Siple for sure. A coach is supposed to be firm, fair, and consistent. I gave baseball a pass the next year.

Springtime came to the Shenandoah Valley and as on most college campuses, the end of winter and the warming weather put the students in the mood to get outside and enjoy the fresh air. Of course, the big farm right across the street from the college brought its own particular air quality! There is nothing quite like the smell of the Shenandoah Valley in late spring. Phew!

Now if you thought because Bridgewater was the first private coed college in Virginia, (1880) that campus life would be progressive, you would be dead wrong. There was the rule that forbid female students from wearing shorts on campus. Really? Yes. It was common to see girls walking across campus with trench coats on in the heat of the day on their way to gym class. Then there was the real kicker. It was a five dollar fine if you were a guy and were caught wearing shoes with no socks. What were these people thinking? The prep style in those days was for guys to wear Bass Weejuns (loafers) with no socks, but at BC it was no go on styling. When the warm weather hit and the five dollar fines started being meted out, we got pretty upset about it.

162

Some girls in Rebecca Hall were tired of the shorts rule, and it wasn't long before plans were hatched to stage a protest. On the same day, big banners were hung out of the windows of both Rebecca and Wardo. The girls' sign read, "Girls, faculty says down with your shorts!" I helped with the two banners hung from Wardo Hall. One read, "Bridgewater Socks" with the top half of the "o" just having a half moon of dots, . . . This made the banner look from a distance like Bridgewater Sucks! You couldn't see the dots closing the "o" until you got up close to the banner. By far my favorite though, and one of the classic protest signs of all time, was the one we hung that read, CHRIST DIDN'T WEAR SOCKS!

The administration got the message, and these rules were soon changed. Now some people might say I knew what the rules were when I signed on to attend Bridgewater, so I should just accept them. These people are dead wrong, and that kind of thinking leads to blindly accepting the status quo, where nothing gets changed. I think rules and standards should be grounded in reality and common sense, and I have challenged many situations in my life that didn't make sense to me. It didn't always go my way when asking the question," Why," or "Why" not, but often my standing up for what I believed in made a positive difference in the long run. So, my advice is this: Follow your heart and your instincts. In other words, do what you think is right—another lesson I learned at Boys Home.

The first time I drove a car, my friend and I were returning to the Bridgewater College campus from the Harrisonburg truck stop. It was a beautiful spring Saturday night, and we had dropped our dates off so they could get back to their dorm by curfew. This was in 1964, and girls had a curfew at Bridgewater, guys did not. Ted and I were hungry, so we headed back to town, where the only place open at eleven-thirty p.m. in those days was the truck stop. We had borrowed the car from a fellow baseball teammate, and I wanted to drive it back.

Even though I was twenty at the time, I had never learned to drive at Boys Home, and didn't have a driver's license. With no access to a car at the

Home, I really saw no need to learn to drive. Although we had downed a couple of beers earlier in the evening, it was just plain inexperience that led to the accident. I was going just a wee bit too fast when I started turning left into the campus entrance. The car hit some gravel and I panicked! I'm not sure I even hit the brakes as we skidded toward the right of the two large brick columns that framed the road to the parking lot. Boom! The impact knocked the right column back about two feet, although it didn't fall over. Thankfully me and my buddy were alright. I was pretty much in shock when the first of the girls from the nearby dorm came running up. The police showed up a while later and gave me a couple of tickets. No license, reckless driving. The car was totaled, frame bent, or so the owner said a couple of days later. He was very mad, and I didn't blame him for that. It was a stupid move on my part.

He said he didn't have insurance, (knowing what I know today, I'm not sure if that was true) and I promised to repay him. It took me a summer and a half of making $1.25 an hour, which was still the minimum wage, to repay my debt. That was a tough life's lesson. Coach Siple came to Bridgewater to talk to the judge on my behalf when my court date came up. He brought Dimick with him, as Pete was already back from his freshman year of college. I got off easy, and Redeye and I had a pretty good laugh over the whole thing.

I was to see Pete one more time before he passed at an early age. In June of 1981, we met in Covington for the seventy-fifth anniversary of the founding of Boys Home. We spent the weekend together with our families at a local motel. We were both married with two kids, and he got to meet his namesake, my son Pete! Six weeks later, Donald Darwin Dimick, my brother from another mother, died of a heart attack. RIP Redeye, we will meet again

It had been a rough year, but I survived it. Once again, my grades were just good enough to keep me eligible to play basketball next season. I was playing with fire. My emotional issues had burst forth on several occasions, and, as I said earlier, that had cost me a spot on the Eagles Varsity basketball team. I was basically trying to paddle the canoe with just my hands. There were some good things too; I had met Pat, and Betty Kline had become an ear and a confidant. All in all, I give myself a 1.9, which is what my GPA was!

Unchained

28

I AM A ROCK—I AM AN ISLAND

I worked as a playground director in Covington during the summer and loved it. I had a way with kids, and when school picked up in the fall, I could see myself as a P.E. teacher and coach one day. I moved from Wardo to Wright East, and my roommate and fellow basketball teammate Jim Ellis became a lifelong friend. "Stick" could "ball"! I gave him that nickname because he was six-foot-four and thin as a rail. He had transferred in, and so was not eligible to play the first semester in conference games, but when he hit the floor, he became an instant standout. He was from Arlington, Virginia, and had played on a state championship team with our point guard Jim Hawley.

Another great player and lifelong friend who lived on our floor was Jim Upperman, who went on to score over two thousand points in his career at Bridgewater. Things were looking up for the hoops team. I patched things up with Shifty and was able to contribute more and more as the season progressed, coming in off the bench. The future was looking bright.

Pat and I had a roller coaster relationship, and one spring evening we tried to elope, but as with most things about our romance, it didn't work out so well. We were out one weekend, maybe at a cabin party or dance, and in our inebriated and euphoric state, decided to head to North Carolina to get married! We went back to campus and picked up Stick and another friend, Mark Clary. The three-and-a-half-hour drive to Greensboro was lots of fun, talking and blasting Motown on the radio, but the ride back was a real downer. We found out there was a twenty-four-hour waiting period, which meant our marriage balloon had been burst. It was a somber crew as we drove back to Bridgewater with our tails between our legs.

In 1964, the United States became more heavily involved in the Vietnam War. We had gotten involved in the late 1950s, with the "Domino Theory" foreshadowing the spread of communism. I didn't know it in September '65, when I started my junior year, but Vietnam was going to play a big part in my future.

School started off bad and got quickly worse. Same old lack of study habits, same off and on relationship with Pat, but the kicker was that I was not playing basketball. Coach Myers had instituted a timed mile run as a prerequisite for making the team. I didn't train, and I didn't make the time. Totally my fault. Shifty said I could start on the JV team, but I was done.

The rest of the semester was a blur, as I was totally lost at sea. As the popular song by Martha and the Vandellas said, "Nowhere to run to, baby, nowhere to hide." I went to the Walkers in Norfolk for solace at the end of the semester. I didn't even take exams.

I was certainly in a dark hole. For the first time in my life, I was feeling sorry for myself. And I had brought it all on by my lack of self-discipline.

When I got to Norfolk for Christmas and told the Walkers I wasn't going back to school, Etta was kind of lukewarm about the idea of me staying with them. She was upset with me and couldn't understand why I wasn't returning to BC. I finally had to tell her the whole truth, that I was basically flunking out, and going back for exams was not going to change that fact.

I was struggling for sure, and then this song, *I Am a Rock*, by Simon and Garfunkel was released and helped firm me up. It stiffened my backbone in some way, and I sang it to myself as an act of defiance; I was going to make it on my own. I didn't need anybody else: A rock doesn't feel pain or cry, it stands firm in the face of adversity.

With this stoic resolve, I decided to join the Army because I was worried I would be drafted. It was not an all-volunteer force in those days. College students were exempt from the draft, so when I left Bridgewater, I was fair game for Uncle Sam. If I was drafted, I would be made to serve a two-year commitment, with a good chance I would become an infantryman serving in Vietnam. I sure didn't want that, so I enlisted, which meant a three-year hitch. But because I had enlisted, I could pick my MOS (military occupational specialty) if I qualified.

I could type a little, so I signed up to be a clerk. I got a job in a small manufacturing outfit making aluminum storm windows and doors until my induction date in March. My two months there, making the minimum wage of $1.25 an hour, were quite instructive, and would make a funny story all by itself. These were "salt of the earth" folks, and believe me, it got quite salty on their interactions!

So, on a Saturday in March of 1966, I found myself with at least a hundred and fifty other guys at the induction station in Richmond, Virginia. We were in this huge room, and they would call us out for physicals, etc. I quickly got tired of just sitting around, and by mid-afternoon I was worn out from talking to guys I might not ever see again.

All of a sudden, this big Marine Sergeant burst into the room accompanied by a couple of Corporals. He was in his dress uniform and had stripes all up and down his arm. Very imposing. He cut his eyes and arm towards a group of guys who had been drafted, and told them to follow him, that they were now Marines! There was definitely an OMG! moment from everyone in the room, and as they all walked out, I breathed a sigh of relief. I later found out that this was an exception, that there were very few drafted who went into the Marines, and that because I had enlisted there was no chance of me becoming "one of the few."

After a box dinner, we boarded a train headed south to Fort Jackson, South Carolina.

29

YOU'RE IN THE ARMY NOW

There was a lot of nervous excitement on the train on the way to Columbia, South Carolina, so most of us didn't sleep a lot. Lots of guys playing cards and talking smack, even some bragging about what they would do to "Charlie." I thought well, I could hit him over the head with my typewriter.

The Army had it all planned out. We got there just in time for breakfast, and then it was time for haircuts. Down to the nub. This was the era of long hair, and there were some sad eyes and near tears on plenty of the guys. The rest of the day was typical Army: hurry up and wait. Which means you jog somewhere like it's the end of the world, then you sit or stand around forever.

We got the olive drab duffle bag; the clothes, socks, and even our underwear was green. Preparing for the jungle! They kept us busy for the rest of the day and that night put us into temporary sleeping quarters. When we bedded down for the night, I was whipped.

I had been informed that I was on "fire duty" from two to three a.m. This is pretend guard duty with no weapon. A guy tapped me on the shoulder for my shift and I began to walk back and forth in the barracks as instructed. After a few minutes I thought, "Why walk? I can just lean against this post and see everything that was going on," which was a bunch of guys sleeping and snoring.

I looked at an empty bunk near me with loving eyes, and soon found myself lying there thinking, "I'll just rest my eyes for a couple of minutes, then I'll get up and resume my duty." The Sergeant woke me with a shout and said we were at war, and someone who fell asleep on guard duty could be shot! It didn't matter that we weren't in Nam! That got my attention, to say the least.

The Army was a game changer for me. Guys from all over the country with various educational backgrounds, skin color, and views on everything, gave me a much broader perspective on life. As the focus of my life turned away from sports, I began to exhibit more self-discipline, and the Army gave me a chance to hone my leadership skills.

I had seen Pat only sporadically since I left school and neither of us were letter writers, although we did talk on the phone frequently. I wasn't sure where our relationship was headed, especially with me now in the Army. I did the usual eight weeks of basic training and was assigned to stay at Fort Jackson for ten weeks of Advanced Individual Training (AIT). Clerk school. Meanwhile, I was pining for Pat, and waited endless hours in line to call her on the PX (post exchange) phone.

I wasn't always able to reach her, and so I drank many a pitcher of beer commiserating with my fellow soldiers. I was pitching for the company fast pitch softball team, and our Company Commander took a shine to me. I was able to wrangle a three-day pass from him around the Fourth of July. I can't remember the exact dates. I caught the Greyhound and headed to Baltimore, as Pat lived in Towson. From the bus stop, I cabbed it to her house.

Her mom said she was at work, so I walked down to the local Shoney's Big Boy, where Pat was a stellar waitress. It was all excitement as I walked in straight and sharp in my dress uniform, and the whole place stood and cheered as we embraced! After that welcome, it was an easy sell to get Pat to agree to elope, and before we knew it, we were in front of a Justice of the

Peace, married, and headed to Virginia Beach for a quick two-day honeymoon.

Pat's parents were livid when we returned, so angry with me! At this point, I was already AWOL, Absent Without Leave, which was not good, especially during wartime. I could have been put in jail for that. Luckily, I got in contact with my CO, and he cut me a big break by extending my pass for another four days!

I pitched my butt off for him when I got back. I'm not sold on astrology, but my Spirit of Aries plaque says, "can become hasty and impatient." That was true for me in my relationship with Pat Kloes! But I was now married, and, in a subconscious way, it settled me down and made me more responsible.

After I had finished eight weeks of basic training, and another ten weeks of learning the ropes of being an Army clerk, in Fort Jackson, I spent five weeks at Fort Benjamin Harrison, Indiana. It was nicknamed "Uncle Ben's Rest Home" because life there was so easy it hardly seemed like it was associated with the military.

At Uncle Ben's, I got more advanced clerical training, particularly dealing with personnel recordkeeping. From there I was assigned to Fort Leonard Wood, Missouri, where I arrived just in time to try out for the post basketball team. I never did any clerk duty there. I was playing the best basketball of my life and made the team. But we were so loaded. I was the eighth or ninth man and spent a lot of time clapping and rooting for my teammates. For example, our center, a six-foot-eight jumping jack and shot blocker, played with Willis Reed at Grambling State University. Reed later had a Hall of Fame career with the New York Knicks, and was voted in 1997 as one of the fifty top NBA players of all time.

I was assigned TDY (temporary duty) and spent the winter traveling around the Midwest playing basketball against other Army teams. It was gravy. Most of the time we didn't even wear uniforms. Lots of former college players, and some future pro players, made for some exciting contests. My name showed up on a roster to head for Nam in December 1966, but my coach got me deferred until our season was almost over. They gave me a thirty-day leave to visit with Pat, and before I knew it, I was headed to a combat zone!

30

VIETNAM

I ducked as the sniper fire whizzed overhead. The rest of the guys paid it no mind and just kept on playing basketball. It was near twilight during my first couple of weeks in Vietnam, and I was still learning the ropes. I had flown out of Dulles Airport on my first airplane ride about three weeks before, in March 1967. After a few days in Fort Ord, California, I was issued all new clothing and boots. I boarded a troop transport plane with a big crowd of enlisted men, and after a stop to refuel in Alaska, we put down umpteen hours later at Ben Hua Air Force Base, about twenty miles from Saigon. It was a long flight, giving me a chance to think about what the hell I had gotten myself into.

After a night at Ben Hua, they put me on a truck and told me I was assigned to the First Infantry Division. We rolled up to the Big Red One headquarters base camp, in Dian (pronounced Zion), where the sign at the entrance read, "No Mission Too Difficult, No Sacrifice Too Great—Duty First!" I thought to myself, "Oh sh.., I'm going to die here!"

We got there too late in the evening for dinner at the chow hall, so they sent us over to the closest PX to get something to eat. I was sitting there having a sandwich and a beer when I heard a familiar voice call out, "Nunnally!" I turned around and it was my buddy Tommy, whom I had befriended at Fort Jackson in AIT. We had hung out and played a lot of hoops and poker together. I had lost track of him and had no idea he was in

Nam. He had shipped out right after AIT and so had been in-country about eight months already.

We caught up over a couple of more beers and Tommy asked me if I had been assigned to a unit yet. I said no but that I was expecting to be a "morning report" clerk for one of the infantry units in the field, a job that I wasn't too excited about. Tommy was working in the division records keeping office, and he said he would take me to his Commanding Officer and see if they could use me. I was cool with that, and that night I met the CO, and he said sure, they could find a spot for me. They put me in a "hooch" (barracks) that night, and the next day I started working in the personnel records department for all E1–E6 enlisted men in the Big Red One.

Naturally I started asking where the best after hours basketball game could be found, which was why I found myself ducking from sniper fire. All the guys laughed and told me to relax. The pick-up games were played on an outside court near the perimeter of the base camp. The camp perimeter was a big circle with sandbagged bunkers spaced evenly for protection from Charlie.

Agent Orange (that nasty herbicide that caused many illnesses and deaths to our troops and the friendly Vietnamese) had been used to clear about five hundred yards of all living vegetation. Just beyond that was the jungle and trees. The sniper was in the trees firing toward us while we played basketball, but never even came close to hitting anyone, so he was left alone. It was surmised that he was not a regular fighter, just someone from the nearby village who had been ordered by the Viet Cong (VC) to be a sniper a couple of times a week. He shot his allocated number of rounds, climbed down from his perch, and went home.

I said we could easily take him out so why not kill him. Easy answer, I was told; if we killed him the VC might put someone up there who would actually shoot someone! So, it was a case of live and let live. After a bit, the afternoon shots from the trees ceased, and no one really gave it any more thought.

My time in Nam was a little like the TV sitcom M*A*S*H. Lots of funny stuff happening right in the middle of a war.

I'm not sure if I played a part in the killing. I know I fired my weapon with a few short bursts, but I really couldn't see Charlie.

So how did a clerk end up out on a night patrol firing a machine gun for the Big Red One? As a trainee in eight weeks of basic training at Fort Jackson, I learned to disassemble, assemble, and shoot the M14. Initially I was not a good shot, and our Drill Sergeant kept telling me I was going to "bolo," which meant I was no good. I couldn't shoot even at a minimum level. If this happened, I was warned, I would have to repeat basic training. What made matters worse, I was the Assistant Platoon Guide, a position of leadership. As it turned out, the day we were going to qualify on the M14, it was lightly raining. By luck and the Grace of God I not only qualified, but I hit enough targets to be considered an expert. I remember I had to blow the water out of my peep sight just before I squeezed off the last round that found its mark. They even gave me something to wear on my dress uniform to prove it.

When I hit Nam, I was given a very minimum training on the M60 machine gun. It was a heavy weapon with a lot of firepower, the kind that fires the bullets fed in with the bandolier, which held a hundred rounds. You typically had to rest it on the ground to fire with any accuracy, although Rambo held it as his side in the movie with the same name. When I proudly told one of my buddies I was going to tote the M60, he basically said, "Dude, if you value your life, don't ever fire that thing!" I said sure I would, the M60 was the baddest thing we took on patrol! He said," That's the point rookie, Charlie will try and take out the machine gun first!"

The reason I had to train on the M60 in the first place was that the Commanding General had decided that all members of the Big Red One should be put in harm's way and do some fighting. I'm sure he thought it would boost morale among the troops, especially the "grunts" (Infantrymen).

Basically, I would be asked to go out on night ambush patrol once a month. The very thought of that scared the crap out of me! I was a lover, not a fighter. Sure enough my name came down on the duty roster three weeks or so after I joined the post. I was about to participate in my first patrol. Man, how I was dreading that day. Meanwhile, I was trying to get as much practice with the M60 as I could, and looking at the roster to try and figure out who I could get to be my ammo bearer. I wanted a big dude. Trouble was, they didn't want to waste the ammo on practice with a clerk pulling the trigger.

There were about twenty of us who assembled at dusk for the night ambush patrol. It was my first one, and I was curious and scared as we walked into the jungle just past the perimeter. We were spaced a few yards apart in an "L" shaped formation, facing a known VC travel route. I was wide eyed and alert, but as it got dark, I noticed some guys nodding off. About one a.m., the firing started. For thirty seconds or so, everyone was firing in the same direction, with no incoming fire. Every fifth round was a tracer bullet, with a red light to show where the bullets were going. I joined in with a few quick bursts, then remembered what my friend said and took my hand off the trigger. The firing stopped and it stayed quiet for the rest of the night. At daybreak we all walked out and found a what remained of a water buffalo blown to bits!

31

ENTERPRISING VENTURE

Just before I left Vietnam, I sold my share of the enterprise for a tidy sum. It had been my idea, but I had to have a couple of partners to help with all of the logistics of running a small business, so I recruited a couple of guys who said they could use some extra cash. It wasn't an official business of course, that would have been against regulations. It was allowed because it helped boost morale.

I had been working in the record's unit of the 1st Infantry Division for a few months and had recently been put in charge. Our unit processed the records of all incoming and outgoing enlisted men, rank E1–E6 in the Big Red One. There were over five thousand men in the division who fell into that category at any one time, so we were kept busy. In the Army in the days before computers, you hand-carried your official records with you when you went from one duty station to the next. Included in the large folder were personnel records, financial records, and medical records, basically a history of a soldier's time in service. The processing was the typical Army hurry up and wait, with the guys spending most of the day sitting around in the low-slung building we called an office, waiting for their name to be called.

It was hot and muggy in that building, and the guys would get plenty thirsty. The only water available was outside in these canvas bags that held large quantities of warm water. The water was accessed by several spigots circling the canvas bag. I began to put my plan into place shortly after I was made a temporary NCOIC, the non-commissioned-officer-in-charge. (I couldn't be made a Sargent because I didn't have the right training.) I thought, "Why not offer the troops something other than that tepid water to drink?" It could boost morale and make a little cash on the side as well. We were over a mile away from the closest PX, so there was nowhere for the guys to get a cold drink.

I went to the officer in charge, Captain Jones, and told him my idea, which was to offer sodas and beer to the guys while they were waiting to be processed. We would put the cans on ice in coolers and sell them for twenty-five cents. He was hesitant to approve, but I asked him to just give it a trial period and see how it worked. He gave the OK and we went to work.

We went to the nearby village and bought coolers made of recycled beer and soda cans, and arranged to have blocks of ice delivered each day. We walked to the PX after work and we each carried two cases of drinks back to our office. The next morning, we iced down the goods and we were in business. We sold out the six cases well before lunchtime! I was very excited that this seemed to be working, so we walked to the PX at lunch time and carried back six more cases. Sold those out in about sixty minutes!

It went this way for a few more days and then Capt. Jones said we would have to shut the operation down! Bummer! It seems a couple of the guys in the finance department had gotten sick after drinking sodas, and the folks in the infirmary were thinking the ice was being made from contaminated water. This was not good. We had been having fun and were making a tidy profit of fifteen cents per can. They only cost us ten cents each, (I guess the Army was subsidizing them) and we were selling them for twenty-five. I thought about possible solutions and Bingo, it hit me! I asked the Captain if we could continue to sell if we used refrigerators instead of ice and he said, "Sure. Why not."

That Saturday we headed to Saigon, about twenty miles away, and bought three huge refrigerators. My partners and I spent the night in a nice hotel and availed ourselves of some good food and nightlife. The next day we managed to hook a ride back to the base camp on a big truck and off-loaded our new refrigerators. We were back in business!

Word got out and we were soon selling ice cold beverages to soldiers who lived on base as well as those passing through. We had so much business we started paying a 2nd Lieutenant twenty dollars a day to use his truck during lunchtime to go to the PX to get beer and sodas. When I left Nam, we were up to twenty-five to thirty cases a day, and we were all making more money per month than our Army pay—even including the $125 per month we received for combat pay.

So, ask me why I didn't become an entrepreneur when I got out of college? I think I could have done quite well in the business world, but making money could never have replaced the fun, joy, and satisfaction I would get from being a teacher and coach. No amount of dollars could replace those experiences.

I want to emphasize that in wartime, lots of different folks have lots of different experiences. I was one of the lucky ones called support personnel. They used to say it took eight support personnel to keep one infantryman in the field fighting. I honor all my brothers who fought, were injured, or gave their lives in Vietnam, and I yearn for the day when all of God's children can live in harmony and peace, in accordance with His plan. Amen.

"Nunnally, get your ass back to work." That's the message the new officer in charge of the Records Department for the 1st Infantry Division had sent to me. I was playing tennis at the time, instead of being in the office. I had been in Nam for 355 days, and I was waiting for my official orders to be cut so I could head back to the States. Of course, I already knew where I was going, as I had sent myself to Fort Meade, Maryland, halfway up the Washington-Baltimore Parkway.

Pat was from Baltimore and had graduated from Bridgewater in June 1967. She was teaching P.E. at a junior high in nearby Broadway and was living in Bridgewater. I knew Pat would want to be spending some weekends with her family back in Baltimore, so I had arranged to be sent to Fort Meade.

Now, you must be asking yourself how I did that, right? Easy! My buddy Tommy, who had basically gotten me the job in the Division Records Department when I arrived in Vietnam, had left about four months after I got there. He was assigned to the 35th Artillery Brigade at Fort Meade. We had the same rank, had basically the same training, so our MOS (Military Occupational Specialty) was the same. So, what I did was take a copy of his reassignment orders and replace his name with mine, changing out the serial numbers, etc.

The regulations stated that an officer had to sign copies of orders to make them official, and with over five thousand soldiers' records to process and take care of, we generated over a hundred sets of orders a day. We took them to a 2nd Lieutenant, whose only job was to look over the orders and sign them. Now the Lieutenant didn't really know squat about the details of what was in each order, so he pretended to look them over and put his signature on them. It was so funny the day I took my orders for him to sign. He was like, "Wow, that's a great assignment you got there, Nunnally." I said something like, "Just lucky" and laughed all the way back to my desk!

The new Officer in charge and I didn't get along from the start. In my experience, a lot of Officers didn't know a whole lot about what really was going on, the real leading was done by the Sergeants in the Army. And the real work and fighting was mostly done by the lower ranks. This guy was no exception, and to make matters worse, he didn't know what he didn't know. At least he wasn't leading men out in the jungle. But when he sent his lackey for me, I got ticked off and told the guy to tell the Officer I was "short," which meant I had a short time left in Vietnam. He sent me back a note saying he was giving me a direct order to show up to work, which I had to obey or face the consequences. (Here we are again with "Because I said so.")

They really didn't need me there; the new guy was just making a power play to show everyone he was the boss. He had just taken over from Captain J.R. David, who left in February, about a month before I rotated back to the States. That's not really the way to get the loyalty and the best effort of your subordinates, and that Officer was going to get a lesson in leadership a little later. Now, it's a court-martial offense to disobey a direct order from an Officer, so I spent four more days working before I flew out. You can bet I wasn't going to forget that guy.

My one-year paid vacation to Southeast Asia was over! I was coming along. Getting back to what I had learned from my mentors at Boys Home. I'll humbly present to you a letter of commendation from CPT David when he left, dated 16 February 1968.

> As the non-commissioned officer responsible for the administrative processing of all newly arriving and departing E1 thru E6 personnel for the Division, you manifested a degree of competency and confidence not normally attained by much older and more experienced non-commissioned officers. Your aggressiveness, sense of urgency, and initiative were directly instrumental in the always professional performance of the Processing Unit.

> Your success in winning the loyal cooperation of your men has been your most significant achievement.

You may recall with deep pride the cohesive efficiency of your Unit. It has been a pleasure serving with you.

> J R David
> CPT, AGC
> Chief, Personnel Records
> Branch

I arrived at the 35th Artillery Brigade at Fort Meade and got assigned to an inspection team that checked on the readiness of all the Nike Missile sites in the Baltimore/Washington/Hampton Roads area. My job was to check to make sure that all the personnel records of the guys assigned to the units were up to snuff, particularly the security clearances. They all had a form of Top-Secret clearances due to the sensitive nature of the missile site.

On one trip, we went to Fort Story, near Virginia Beach, Virginia. I was familiar with the area because I used to play with our dogs on the large sand dunes near there when I was a boy living in Norfolk. So, I walked into the office where the personnel records were kept, and who do I see first? The Officer who gave me a hard time in Nam! He was now in charge of a part of their operation, which included their records. I didn't mention our time together in Vietnam, but I went over those records with a fine-tooth comb, and he spent a couple of late evenings with his clerk bringing a huge pile of files up to date. I slapped him with a couple of negative comments on my written report too. I have observed that when as a leader you show genuine care and concern for others, they will follow you anywhere, and will remain loyal to you and your cause through thick and thin.

32

WHEN YOU COME TO A FORK IN THE ROAD, TAKE IT

I had big decisions to make. What's next after the Army? Could I even get back into Bridgewater if I wanted to? After two and a half years there, I had a 1.535 GPA out of a possible 4.0. Pat encouraged me to try and get back in. So, when I visited and basically begged, told them I was a changed man, showed them the above letter of commendation, by the grace of God I was now an Eagle again!

I had enlisted in March of '69 for three years, but the Army let me slide the last three months so I could return to school for the second semester of '69. I really was a changed man—those had not been just words! My main concern now was my studies and learning how to be a married man. I had to have a 2.0 GPA to graduate, which meant I needed to make the Dean's List every semester. It took a 3.5 GPA to make the Dean's List, so I had my work cut out for me. I think the first semester back I made almost all A's, and that impressed the physical education faculty.

Pat and I settled into the roles of married life and had a small apartment in Bridgewater. She had her teaching salary and I had money from the GI bill, so we were okay financially. I took two P.E. classes in the summer, thanks to Professor Laura Mapp. She went out of her way to accommodate me, and I doubt that she was compensated for teaching me one-on-one. I squeezed in one other summer class and aced all three!

I was twenty-five years old when classes started in the fall. An old man for that setting. Add to that the fact that I was now a day student, and that meant I was totally out of the loop on what was happening on campus. Basketball has always been my siren call, and I started going to the gym occasionally. Pat encouraged me: "You know you want to play. Go for it: you are academically eligible now." I wasn't sure, but the returning players were friendly enough, and I had my old coach Shifty for class. I decided to talk with him about it, and he seemed lukewarm to the idea. He let me know that he had all five starters back from the previous year, and he couldn't promise me any playing time.

I had a different attitude this time around. I didn't have anything to prove, just playing for the love of the game. All five starters returned from an 8-14 record the previous season, but with three seniors with four years on the Varsity, the team was poised for a good season. Lo and behold, there was no timed mile! We ended up 14-11, and still hold the team scoring record of 92.1 points per game, with all five returners plus some old man all averaging double figures! We poured in 130 points over Shepherd College, also a record. We played a lot of "hey" defense though; instead of guarding a man tight, we would just holler "hey" as he went up to shoot and hoped he missed!

There was one tragic part of that season though. It was snowing when the charter bus pulled out from campus to head to Richmond. We were going to play Randolph Macon, one of our conference rivals. Normally we took two vans for away games, but the cheerleaders were going along on this trip, so we needed a charter bus.

By the time we reached the foot of Afton Mountain near Waynesboro, there were two to three inches of snow on the ground. We were heading up on Route 250, because Interstate 64 was still under construction. Route 250 was a three-lane roadway, where the middle lane was used for passing.

The white Lincoln crossed two lanes before it hit us! I guess the driver lost control, hit the brakes, and slid into our bus. The impact sent our bus into a sideways skid, and, as there was no guardrail, we were lucky that the bus ended up leaning at an angle against a couple of trees, as we could have very easily rolled over.

The few seconds after the crash, our skidding, and finally being stopped by the trees seemed like an eternity. Everyone was in a bit of shock, especially the bus driver and Coach Myers, who had been sitting directly behind him. Some of us had been playing cards and they flew everywhere. I broke the silence and ice when I quipped, "Damn, I had a good hand too!"

My Army training took over and I was able to help organize getting everyone off the bus and get to a safe spot off to the side of the road. There was an alcohol smell coming from the Lincoln after the crash, and the guy driving was walking around in a daze. The rescue squad came, pried the woman out of the car, and we later found out she had died, maybe immediately or on the way to the hospital. When we went to Richmond to play the Yellow Jackets in a make-up game later that season, they stung us bad and crushed us.

I was taking a class with Professor Jim Reedy, and we hit it off right away. He was a cool guy, a Bridgewater grad who was once one hell of a basketball player. He was also the baseball coach. My grades were still Dean's List, and he said he needed another pitcher for the spring. I was the winning pitcher for a few games that year and helped out as a part time assistant for Jim and the Eagles the following year. He was instrumental in getting me into my next gig. I had a great friendship with Steve Gioielli, who also played on the basketball team with me. Steve was an excellent center fielder and pitcher for the Eagles and played in the heralded Valley League in the summer after his graduation. As it turns out, we were both living up in Northern Virginia a couple of years later and played a lot of golf together. Mo, as we called each other, was destined to be my best man.

During this time, I was coming to the realization that Pat and I were not suited for marriage—at least not to each other. The time we spent apart while I was in the Army just postponed the inevitable. She wanted to head to Baltimore every weekend—and did so many times by herself when I had a basketball or baseball game. In addition, she would never come on campus to see me play. Something was off with that, but she didn't want to talk about it.

I knew that she had a girl staying with her for a time while I was overseas, and I had heard some other rumors. It was obvious to me that we were incompatible for the long run. Our outlook on life and people was just so different. She had no faith history and did not believe in God. I hung in there as long as I could, but after talking with Betty Kline, I decided to leave Pat. She was not for the split at first, but after a while, she came to realize it was the best thing to do for both of us.

I moved in with the Klines to finish out the school year. They lived just outside of Bridgewater in a house built in the woods that Paul designed. I loved that house! I had a room in the basement, and those three months I lived with them were very therapeutic and just what I needed. We spent time at the local pool when it opened, with me playing and splashing around with the three kids.

Betty told me years later that a friend of hers who saw me at the pool with them came up to her and said she didn't realize that they (Betty and Paul) had another son. Betty just replied, "Oh yeah, that's Mike."

Pat moved back to Baltimore when her teaching job was over. I loved her then, and still love and cherish the memory of her. She went to work for the Social Security Administration and retired from there in '95. I went up to Baltimore and met her in a bar just one time, and we both cried as we hugged goodbye. We never communicated again, though I often thought of her. I got a call from her younger brother sometime after she passed from cancer in 2005 at the age of sixty. Rest in Peace Pat.

This hurts my heart to write . . .

As I look back at this time in my life, I have to ask: Where was God in my life? I hadn't been to church in quite a while if you don't count chapel at the college. In this regard, I was like most young people my age. (I wasn't thinking about that question of where God was then, but I did think about it later when I started attending St James Episcopal Church in Leesburg, Virginia.) I was a 'believer." Even though I wasn't attending church, I feel that for the most part I was living a Christian life. I was trying to do the right thing by my fellow man. At Church of the Ascension in Norfolk, and continuing at Emanuel Episcopal Church in Covington, and chapel at Boys Home, I had learned the creeds, Ten Commandments, and basic tenets of the Episcopal Church. These weren't at the forefront of my thoughts and actions, but were layered in my subconscious, helping me to try and make the right choices. I tried to treat people as I would like to be treated. I prayed to God in my mind many times to continue to protect me.

Of course, there were plenty of times I fell short, but I paid the price and moved on. I came to realize that God was always there and active in my life, in the form of the angels he sent my way: My sister, Celia, who introduced me to the Episcopal Church; Reverend Rose and Virginia Danner, from Church of the Ascension in Norfolk; Boys Home and my mentors there, Bob Burrowes, Granny Myers, and most especially Paul Siple, who was my coach, role model, and father figure, and Betty and Paul Kline, who made me a de facto member of their family. And yes, Pete Dimick, my brother from another mother!

Unchained

33

GRADUATE SCHOOL

Graduation from Bridgewater was on the horizon, and again it was: What's next? I have never had some kind of grand plan for my life; mostly I have just made decisions when I came to a fork in the road.

Reedy called me into his office in late spring and told me about an opportunity that had presented itself at Madison College (now James Madison University) in nearby Harrisonburg. Madison, which had long been primarily a women's teaching college, was going to start admitting men. They had an opening in the physical education department for a graduate teaching position, whereby someone could teach P.E. to freshmen, while at the same time attending graduate school to earn a Master of Science in P.E. Jim said he would recommend me for the position and felt Ms. Mapp would throw her weight behind me also.

I was very much worried about the fact that my overall GPA would seriously hurt my chances, but Reedy said my Dean's List efforts since I returned would certainly carry the most weight. I interviewed with Dr. Marilyn Crawford, the P.E. department head, and went from flunking out at Bridgewater to full professor status at Madison! My initial reaction to Dr. Crawford was that she was a firm, no nonsense kind of person, although I did see her smile on occasion. As I got to know her a little better, she warmed up to me, but still kept her distance. I was in her office as she was giving me instructions on my teaching assignments, and she said I had full status as a professor except for the caveat about dating. I was not allowed to date my own students, for obvious reasons. I wasn't worried about that, as there were about a thousand males and three thousand females on the campus. I liked my odds!

I began taking graduate classes in June, and signed up for a summer intramural men's basketball league that was forming. We ended up with about five or six teams in the league. I recruited Jimmy Dixon, a basketball team member with the Eagles, and we filled out the roster with some random sign-ups. The games started and it was soon apparent that we had the best team in the league, although most of the games were competitive. Just before the season-ending tournament, an incident occurred that tested my convictions and ended up putting me in a perilous spot.

The commissioner of the league was a young professor, Dr. Lipton, who also taught in the P.E. department. (They always admonished me to call it physical education, as it was more "professional" sounding, but what the hell, it was—and is—P.E. to most people) Now, I saw quite a bit of Dr. Lipton that summer, as he was the professor in some administrative course I was taking, was the commissioner of the basketball league, and was a player on one of the teams. Frankly, I didn't like the guy. I thought he was an arrogant man, with a huge case of "little man syndrome."

The trouble started when we were playing a game against the team Lipton was on. He was a feisty little guard, as was Jimmy. They were guarding each other, and during the course of the game Lipton began talking smack to Jimmy, and it was returned in kind. Their play became more and more physical against each other, but really nothing out of the ordinary for an intramural league. On one particular play, Jimmy drove to the hoop and Dr. Lipton gave him a real hard foul. Jimmy said something like ". . . Doc, get the . . . off me!"

Dr. Lipton kicked Jimmy out of the game on the spot, and then when Jimmy gave him some back talk, Lipton said he was out of the league as well. I was hot to say the least! I went to his office the next day and said that he had no right to deal out that kind of punishment to a player while he was part of the problem on the floor. The refs hadn't thrown Jimmy out of the game for cursing, as this language was not entirely unusual in the heat of battle. I pointed out that he, Dr. Lipton, had been cursing too.

My pleas fell on deaf ears, and Lipton held his ground. I said, "Fine, then, our team has voted to drop out of the league if Jimmy isn't reinstated." We did drop out, and as word spread about the incident, the whole league folded! This all happened near the end of the class I was taking that Dr. Lipton was teaching, and it definitely affected his attitude toward me.

I really hadn't put a whole lot of effort into the class, as I didn't like the guy, and I was taking two other graduate classes as well. Final grades came out and were posted on his office door, as was the custom then. As I looked at the grades, I couldn't believe it. I had qualified for a B in the class, but he had given me only a C+! I went to his office and basically said there must have been some mistake, that there were students who had lower marks than I did who got B's, but I got a C+.

He smirked and said that it was no mistake, he didn't like my attitude and he could give me any grade he wanted. I couldn't believe he was so brazen. I immediately went to see Dr. Crawford and explained the situation, confident that she would rectify the partiality Dr. Lipton was exhibiting. Nope. She said that she was sorry but there was nothing she could do—that it was a professor's prerogative to give whatever grade they wanted.

What? I just couldn't let that stand. You see, I had to get at least a B- in a class in order to get graduate credit, and more importantly, it just wasn't right! The next day I went to some Dean of something or the other and basically told her that if this wasn't rectified, I would go to the student newspaper, and the local radio station, TV station, and newspaper with my story.

It didn't take long for them to change that grade, but you can't go against the powers that be without ruffling feathers. Hell, I have always been willing to stand on principle and fight for what I thought was right. That's what I learned from Coach Siple and Boys Home.

Stick with me here while I return to the present day, May 2023. I have been doing a lot of internet research and making a lot of phone calls to ensure historical accuracy, and in doing so I was shocked to learn something new about Dr. Lipton and Dr Crawford in relation to the story I just told you. It seems that Dr. Crawford decided not to renew Dr. Lipton's contract after his current one was to expire in 1971. One of the main reasons she gave was a letter signed by several female physical education majors. They had attended the basketball game when the altercation between Jimmy and Dr. Lipton occurred, and thought his actions were unsportsmanlike and unbecoming a member of the faculty.

When Dr. Crawford spoke to Lipton about it, he basically blew her off. Lipton filed a grievance regarding his nonrenewal and it was upheld by a faculty panel citing academic freedom, since he was "off duty" during the game. But here's the kicker; the new President of the college offered him a one-year contract at his same salary and told Lipton he would be evaluated again at the end of that year. He did not accept the offer and moved on. So that closes a loop for me as I had always wondered what happened to Dr. Lipton. Now back to September 1970.

My first teaching assignment was an Introduction to Volleyball class that started in September, I showed up for the organizational meeting dressed in the mod seventies style. I wore a huge, floppy chocolate-colored hat that fell off to one side, bell bottomed pants that almost touched the ground, funky shoes, and a patterned dashiki shirt. Of course, I was also sporting long hair with sideburns halfway down my face. (I was just trying this look out, didn't think it really suited me, and quickly went back to my basic preppy style. It was funky alright, but it just wasn't me.) Fifteen girls and three guys were assigned to the class, and I was excited about the start of my teaching career. The rules of volleyball were changing from the kind of backyard game that everyone played, and I was to teach what they called "power volleyball" at the time. It was basically the same game that is played competitively at all levels these days.

I was not a big fan of grading on skills testing and performance in P.E., which was the norm at Madison at the time. I felt then, and still do now, that participation, attitude, and improvement in a particular activity were the best indicators of how a student should be graded. After all, in most sports, the natural athletes are going to be the ones who always perform the best, so they would be the ones who made the A in a class. I decided to do something totally radical, (not unusual for me) and told the students they would all be getting As in the class, no matter what their skill level. In fact, I may have made passing reference to the fact that I would not even be taking attendance. I told them I was going to make every class fun and challenging, so much so that would not want to miss any of the classes. And I did. I was twenty-six at the time. Old and experienced enough to be the boss, (professor), but yet young enough to really relate to them and have fun with them.

I also decided that instead of introducing all the new rules and skills required of power volleyball at the beginning of the class, I would bring them forward one at a time, over a period of a few weeks. I felt that my students would be frustrated if the way they had been playing was changed all at once. They wouldn't be successful and would get discouraged.

Now there was a much more experienced professor who was teaching volleyball at the same time, and she didn't approve of my teaching methods. And she let me know it. Naturally I then challenged her to a class versus class friendly contest at the end of the semester. When it came time for the game, I got my class psyched up as though we were playing in the Olympics. It was no contest! We waxed them big time.

Just before grades were to come out, Dr. Crawford called me into her office. She had gotten wind of my promise to my students that they would all get A's. Dr. Crawford told me that I couldn't just give everyone whatever grade I wanted, that their grades should be based on some criteria. I looked her straight in the eye and repeated to her what she had said to me about the grade Dr. Lipton gave me: That's a professor's prerogative!

34

CHANGING TIMES

The note said, "I want to go to bed with you." We had just come out of the modern dance class when she followed me and called my name. I stopped and she handed me the note, and it was obvious she was nervous about the whole situation. We had only met about two weeks ago, and had never even had a conversation, let alone a date. Modern dance class, you ask? That's right. There was only one course left that was being offered that I could take to finish up my degree that summer, and that was a modern dance class. If I didn't take and pass that class, I would have to return to school in the fall. After having been in school every month since January 1969, I was ready to be done. But modern dance? I just couldn't see it happening. A friend of mine in grad school, named Wally Carr, was in the same situation. Now Wally was a burly football player who had played for Shepherd College, and I just couldn't see him in tights either.

Nonetheless, over a few beers we decided to give it a shot. The class was going to run only three weeks, with a six-hour-a-day workload. Wally and I showed up for class the first morning to find we were the only males among the fifteen or so students. The professor was a tall, lithesome female in her late thirties or early forties, and she was very excited to have two males in the class. During the morning block, I got my first introduction to Martha Graham and Paul Taylor, and felt pretty stupid in the process. I was about as flexible as a steel beam, and totally felt like a fish out of water. Wally was feeling the same way, and at the lunch break we decided to drop the class and this whole stupid idea.

We went to the professor and told her that there was no way we could possibly continue and pass the course, and that we were not coming back for the afternoon session. She said it was refreshing to have two athletic males in the class, and that she needed us to do some "lifting" in this routine that she had planned for the class presentation to the public, which was to take place as the class finale. By this time, we had let her know that we needed the class to graduate, so she basically told us that if we stuck with it, she could assure us of an A in the course.

Wally and I decided what the hell. We would look foolish, but we wanted that grade. We showed up in tights for the afternoon session and the rest is history! I actually kind of got into it, and during the improvisational part of the public performance, I left the stage, and was dancing in the aisles. Hilarious!

Oh, how times had changed since I graduated from Covington High in June of 1963. In those eight years my little corner of the world had turned upside down, with Vietnam, the British music invasion, Motown, the proliferation of drugs, and the sexual revolution. Things were changing so fast, but there was an aura of innocence about it. The hard reality of overdoses, STDs, and AIDS hadn't set in yet. Heady times.

I read the note, looked at her in her tights and dance garb, and simply responded, "When?"

35

NEXT STEPS

I'm sure you know by now how much I love basketball, and that love has presented me with many opportunities. I was taking a research class during the summer of 1971, and would be graduating soon. The research had to do with foul shooting in basketball, and I needed some subjects to work with.

There was a basketball camp for high school players taking place in Bridgewater's gym, so I was over there almost daily for my course work. During lunch time the coaches running the camp often played some pick-up games, and I joined them on several occasions. One of the coaches, Jerry Hannas, who was coaching at James Wood High School near Winchester, Virginia, knew I was graduating soon and asked me if I had a job yet. I let him know I did not, and he told me that Loudoun Valley High School in Purcellville, Virginia, was looking for a teacher and a coach for the Junior Varsity football team. Me, coach football? I hadn't played since the one year in Youth Football while at Boys Home.

I was just getting into golf, and I took a trip to Bath County near Boys Home to look at a teaching position there. Why? Teachers in the system could play free golf at The Homestead, a resort in Hot Springs that had a very good golf course. They wanted me to teach elementary P.E. in an elementary school cafeteria, and even free golf didn't make that position look attractive.

So, I found myself in Leesburg interviewing for a teaching position at Blue Ridge Middle School in Purcellville and coaching for the Vikings of Loudoun Valley High School. I got the job and started coaching two days later. Blue Ridge was one of three brand new middle schools, and I was to be one of six P.E. teachers.

SECTION FOUR
SPORTS AND TEACHING

Unchained

36

A BOLT OUT OF THE BLUE

It was the first day of new teacher orientation for Loudoun County Public Schools. Loudoun County was growing, and in 1971 the first middle schools were opened: Sterling Middle in the eastern end of the county; J. Lupton Simpson in Leesburg, the county seat; and Blue Ridge in the western end of the county. So many young, excited teachers in the brand spanking new auditorium of JLMS.

I didn't know a soul, and, being a lone wolf, I settled into a seat by myself in the middle of the auditorium, just people-watching before the orientation was to begin. I heard some excited talking and laughing behind me, and as I turned around, there she was! A tall, thin, beautiful young woman wearing a long hippie type dress. She had long brown hair, with two long blond streaks framing her face.

I was totally thunderstruck! I couldn't take my eyes off her and followed her movements as she and the women she was talking to took their seats off to the side and in front of me. I watched her the rest of the day, not paying a whole lot of attention to the various speakers.

The next day I drove to Blue Ridge Middle School to begin my teaching career, and who did I see there? Yep—it was her. How lucky could I get! The first time I spoke to Elaine Margaret Wehle, I made it my life's mission to make her my wife. There was a major problem though, Elaine had a serious relationship at the time.

As we got to know each other, she was constantly talking about the great summer they had together and showed me pictures of them hanging out with friends at the pool, etc. Then I found out he was now in Texas, and that gave me hope. Now I'm not the kind of guy who sweeps women off their feet, but I've always felt that if a woman got to really know me and the chemistry was right, there was a strong possibility that we would get together. So, I decided to play the long game, just getting to know Elaine and her getting to know me. It helped that she was a bit of a sports fan, and a huge Redskins fan. The Skins had a good team in those days, so I always made it a point to head over to Reston, Virginia, on Sundays to watch the game with Elaine and her roommate Karen—usually with a six pack in hand.

Elaine's boyfriend came up a lot in the conversations between them, but I just kept playing it cool. I was head over heels in love and didn't want to blow my chances by getting into those conversations. The Skins had a great year, and we were all fired up about their success. Christmas 1971 was on the horizon and Elaine had a dilemma; she was going to see her boyfriend over the holidays but didn't really have the money to buy him a nice gift. (Salaries were low in those early days.) So I loaned her around a hundred bucks so she could buy my rival a Christmas gift! Again, playing the long game.

During the winter we kind of started going out, without really calling it a date. Elaine was still in contact with her boyfriend, and he was going to visit her at the school in the spring. Elaine was very excited about showing him where she worked, etc. The day came and she walked him down the hall to the gym to meet me. Something very unusual happened as I met him. Elaine left his side, come over to me, put her arm around me and said, "I'd like you to meet my friend, Mike." Boom!

It wasn't too long after that before we became serious about each other and started talking about that engagement ring. It was during a Skins game on a Sunday, and I was hanging out at her apartment. Karen was not around, and Elaine had gone out to get some beer and snacks, so I placed the box with the ring on the TV. When Elaine came back and got settled in, I asked her to turn the sound on the TV up (you had to get up to do that before remote controls), she found the ring, and the rest is history. I don't know if you have ever been thunderstruck, but for me it is the best! Or it could be the worst. I just had to follow my heart.

"And think not you can direct the course of love, for
love, if it finds you worthy, directs your course."
—Kahlil Gibran, 'The Prophet.'

I have been in love a few times in my life, and for me it's not the same as being totally swept off your feet. Elaine did that for me, and we were destined to share a partnership for many years to come. Life has many twists and turns, ups and downs, but you will always love the one who gave you the lightning bolt!

Unchained

37

GROWING AND COACHING

I had a good first year of teaching at Blue Ridge Middle School, although my principal didn't think so. He had been an elementary school principal, and clearly wasn't ready for this assignment. There were too many incidents to mention, but a big one involved a middle school track meet that had been planned for the four new middle schools. It was to be held in the spring, but Mr. K declared that our school would not be participating. Three days before the meet, he was told by the central office that yes, we would be competing.

He called me into his office to give me the news and told me to get it organized on the boy's side. He was always talking to me even though I was not the department head. He didn't like it when I reminded him of that fact. Long story short, he gave me probationary status on my end-of-year evaluation. I felt it was totally bogus and let him know it, but there was nothing I could do about it at the time.

But, ah, during the summer, I learned that he had been either fired or reassigned for reasons unknown to me. I immediately went to the central office and told them I felt my evaluation was based on his dislike for me. I asked them to remove my probationary status because the man who evaluated me was himself incompetent and was fired for it. I'm not sure if they changed my status, but we got a new principal the following year, and lo and behold, she gave me an excellent evaluation!

After that first year of teaching, Elaine and I both got jobs working in the summer at playgrounds with the Department of Parks and Recreation. It was a bit of a drive for her to pick me up, drop me off at a playground at the little hamlet of Saint Louis, Virginia, and then continue to her playground in Round Hill. (She was driving me because I had lost my license due to a couple of "moving violations"—oops!) I was paired up with a young woman named Becky Plaster, and we hit it off right away. I feel like it was sometime in the first week that Becky broke her ankle jumping rope with the kids. Her time on the playground was over, so it was decided that Elaine would join me for the rest of the summer, as she was my driver for a while.

That summer on the playground at Saint Louis was the best. We were the only two white people there the whole summer. Saint Louis was near Middleburg, home of Virginia's horse country, and I believe several of the local families worked in that industry. I can't tell you how enlightening and fun those few weeks were. Early on, we started having cookouts every Friday and the kids loved it.

There was one tough situation though. The cutoff age for the playground was supposed to be fifteen, but there was one young man who kept showing up who I guessed was older. I do so wish I could remember his name. He looked older but we let him join the fun anyway, until he started causing problems with some of the girls. He was a big kid, well put together, and was intimidating to the younger kids.

One morning he was involved in something, and I came up to the group and told him he had to leave the playground, and if he came back, he had to promise to behave and follow the rules. He said, "Whose gonna make me?" I said, "I am." Immediately I heard from several different directions, "He's gonna go home and get his heat!" Which I took to mean his gun! He came back the next day without his "heat," apologized, and added a lot to the group in a positive way the remainder of the summer. On occasion he rode his motorbike and even asked my permission to take Miss Wehle for a short spin. Permission granted.

Despite the probationary evaluation I got at Blue Ridge Middle School in Purcellville in 1972, I knew that teaching/coaching was my calling, and I was damn good at it. I loved kids, and I had a knack for working with them. I coached football for the Vikings in '71, and then I was one of two assistants on the '72 baseball team that won the first State Championship in Loudoun County history! We had a mostly veteran squad, and the head coach, Bootsie Leonard, knew his baseball and his players. The other assistant was a young guy named Archie Moore, who I roomed with for a while. Someone, I'm not sure who, decided that there could only be one assistant coach for baseball going forward, and Archie, the local Loudoun County boy who had attended Shepard College, got the nod.

That was it for me at Blue Ridge. Elaine and I married in June of '73. I transferred to Sterling Middle School in eastern Loudoun the following fall ('73) because of coaching. I liked and respected the Principal at Sterling, Dick Bonieskie. He was a former college athlete himself, so he valued what sports could mean to a school. That was to come in handy when Park View High School opened in 1976, as he was given the principal's job and I joined him there as a member of the P.E. Department.

In the meantime, however, during my three years at Sterling, I coached baseball at nearby Broad Run High School. I was assistant coach in '74, and head coach in '75 and '76. We had some good, coachable ballplayers and won the District Championship in '74 and '76. We came in second in '75, which meant we went on to Regionals for three straight years.

My first year, I was helping Tom Lee, the head coach. He was a nice guy who realized I had a lot to offer as I instituted a firmer direction with the players than they were used to. They responded well for the most part and we were off and running. I particularly loved beating those Loudoun Valley

Vikings in those years because of my history with them, and in fact, that carried over every time the Patriots played them in the future. The last time we played them while I was still coaching, we beat them 12-2 in five innings, as the game was called because of the mercy rule: ahead by ten runs or more. Mercy me!

This poem about coaching was first used by the Wilson Sporting Goods Company in the late sixties. It sums up my teaching philosophy as well.

COACHES NEVER LOSE

A team can lose. Any team can lose. But in a sense a very real sense a coach never loses.

For the job of a coach is over and finished once the starting whistle blows. He knows he's won or lost before play starts.

For a coach has two tasks. The minor one is to teach skills: to teach a boy how to run faster, hit harder, block better, kick farther, jump higher.

The second task, the major task, is to make men out of boys.

It's to teach an attitude of mind. It's to implant character and not simply to impart skills.

It's to teach boys to play fair. This goes without saying.

It's to teach them to be humble in victory and proud in defeat. This goes without saying.

But more importantly it's to teach them to live up to their potential no matter what this potential is.

It's to teach them to do their best and never to be satisfied with what they are but to strive to be as good as they can be if they tried harder.

A coach can never make a great player out of a boy who isn't potentially great. But he can make a great competitor out of any child.

And miraculously he can make a man out of a boy.

For a coach, the final score doesn't read: so many points for my team, so many points for theirs.

Instead, it reads: so many men out of so many boys.

And this is a score that is never published.

And this is the score that he reads to himself and in which he finds his real joy when the last game is over.

It wasn't easy in Loudoun County, though, as I found an entrenched system of top-down authority that seemed bound and determined to hold on to the status quo, especially in sports. Most of the athletic directors and coaches were members of the "good old boy" network, and they didn't seem interested in making any changes to advance their programs. The athletic directors had their own little fiefdoms, and each ruled with an iron hand.

Per usual, I butted heads over the rules and circumstances that didn't make sense to me. It was a fight to get anything changed, or to bring in anything new. One thing I did get for baseball at Park View High School when it opened in 1976 was a pitching machine. I was told there was no money in the budget for a machine and net to use inside, so I convinced the principal to let me sell red, white, and blue ski hats with the slogan "We Are the Patriots" to raise the funds.

Some coaches preferred live pitching for batting practice, but repetition is how a player improves, and a pitching machine can offer up a strike four or five times as fast as a human. It wasn't long before the three other Loudoun high schools followed suit. It took me a long time to get JV baseball started at Park View, but once we had a team and started having success, the other three high schools quickly followed suit.

We played on a dirt infield for years and were at a disadvantage when playing out-of-district teams and in end-of-season playoffs. When an out-of-district team came to play us on our dirt infield, we felt like the country bumpkins—because we were! We wore the same uniforms from '77 then until '85 That's eight years with the same uniform.! We joked that the athletic director must have gotten them on a close out sale, as we had red jerseys with blue pants. You get the idea of how things went.

I pushed and pushed every year for a grass infield, but the answer was always no! It was too much trouble to maintain, etc. The parents wanted it too, and one of the guys asked what he could do to help. He had a truck and I had gotten a good deal from a local sod company, so I took a personal day off from school and we laid down that sod! The baseball coaches and players maintained and manicured that field like it was a major league stadium.

I was teaching at Sterling Middle School and the student versus faculty basketball game was at hand. I was still playing in the men's league at the time and still had game. The day of the contest I came to school on crutches with my ankle wrapped. I told everybody I had sprained my ankle playing in the men's league the night before. The school was buzzing, and the eighth-grade boys were sure they would win. I sat on the bench with the faculty guys and at the half we were down about ten points. A couple of minutes into the third quarter I yelled "Time Out!", stood up, threw my crutches down, unwrapped my ankle, and entered the game laughing! We blew them out going away.

Our first year at Park View in baseball, we were young and not very good. During a game with Valley, I made a couple of defensive moves that didn't pan out, and they were way up on the scoreboard. I told my manager to take off his white T-shirt. I put it on the end of a bat and started waving "we surrender" to the other team!

But here's the most important part, we had some good teams, learned a lot from each other, and made some great memories. As I was writing this memoir, I put a call out to former players and students to send me some of the memories they had on my teams or in my P.E. classes. The snippets in quotes are from my former students and ballplayers. I took the liberty to include a couple of testimonials as well.

> I remember a funny story from health class. Your
> son, I believe, was just born and Jill M. said you must
> be proud, and you replied that you were, but were also
> pretty proud nine months ago! It was how you said it
> that stuck with me as of course all the guys got a good
> laugh out of that.
> —[Student quote]

I know you have heard of the KISS method: Keep It Simple, Stupid. Well, I figured out the K-A method of coaching. Some players are motivated by a coach being tough and hard on them, challenging them all the time to put forth more effort, chastising them for a poor performance, etc. Other players respond to a softer, gentler touch. They want a coach to put his arm around them and tell them how good they are, how much they mean to the team, etc. I developed the K-A method to deal with both types of players. I either "kissed ass" or "kicked ass"!

I coached freshmen basketball at Park View for many years. Now coaching these young guys is a lot different from coaching a varsity team, I had to teach and treat them differently, and really my focus was on teaching them how to be an athlete and team member. As a result, I wasn't as loose and friendly as I was with my baseball teams. We were headed on a long away game trip and one of the players asked if we could stop for food. I said no and with that hit the team with the axiom that became legendary at PV, "a hungry mongoose is a quick mongoose!"

Another time we were playing a pre-season scrimmage at Langley H.S., and I was not pleased with our performance or effort. As we boarded the small bus for the ride back to Sterling, I told the players to stay quiet as we didn't have anything to celebrate. Of course, as they were freshmen, the quiet didn't last long, and as I looked in the rear-view mirror, I saw four or five guys goofing off. I admonished them and again told them to settle down and be quiet.

Sure enough it wasn't long before I looked again and they were quietly laughing and giggling. A couple of minutes later we turned onto Sterling Boulevard. I pulled over and made them get off the bus with their bags and told them to walk the rest of the way back to school. There were shocked looks from the whole team. It was about three quarters of a mile, and I was waiting for them in the locker room when they arrived. Their parents were waiting for them in the parking lot also. Funny thing though, I never heard a word from their parents, and they learned to be quiet when I told them to.

> While walking in from P.E. class, you saw a junior's car in the senior lot. From the sounds of it you had caught this student parking here several times. You may have suggested that a couple us seniors gently press the valve stem and let the air out of his tires. You just kept walking towards the building while we completed the mission. I don't recall ever seeing that car parked there again . . . lol."
>
> —[Student quote]

There were a lot of teachable moments every season. One winter I had a very good team, with no real potential superstars, but as a group they played together and got the most out of their collective ability. They were hard workers who were more mature than the guys I usually coached, so I was able to relax a bit and have fun with them. This incident was not about fun, however. We were headed to play Notre Dame Academy, a private school in nearby Middleburg, Virginia, which had just begun to admit males. It was a ritzy place for these Sterling Park boys, and there were lots of "wows" as we entered the campus. The athletic director met us and showed us the gym and the locker room where we were to dress for the game.

It was apparent to me during warm-ups that their team was way below us in size and skill level, and it became even more apparent when the ref tossed up the ball for the tipoff! We were scoring at will, and even with me subbing in players liberally, we led at the half by something like 42-8. I instructed our players not to try and steal the ball from them in the second half, but to let them shoot uncontested beyond the foul line. I told them that when we got the ball, we had to pass it around five times before we could shoot. We still won by a large margin, and I tried to encourage their young coach to hang in there and keep working hard. As we pulled away headed back to Sterling, I thought to remind myself to tell the new athletic director not to schedule them the next year.

But we did return to Notre Dame just a few short days later. It seems that two or three of our guys had pilfered some of the warm-up jackets from the girl's locker room. The green and gold jackets looked very similar to the University of Notre Dame style, and I guess they couldn't resist. Once I found out about the stealing, I talked to our athletic director and made plans to return the jackets. He wasn't sure when I said I wanted the whole team to go, return the jackets, and apologize, but I insisted.

We called the Sister in charge of the school and made the arrangements. It was a somber ride to Middleburg the next morning, and there were a bunch of hangdog looks, especially among those who stole, as the Sister greeted us. She was gracious as she took the jackets and a written and verbal apology from our captains.

This for me what coaching is about. Teaching life lessons, and hoping they stick. I'm positive Coach Siple would have done the same thing. I still have the letter the Sister wrote, saying that we could come play them again anytime.

Umm, how about the time we played Notre Dame Academy and we 'borrowed' all their Notre Dame sweatpants and sweatshirts out of their lockers after beating them like 75-10. My mom busted our team and we had to ride the short bus back to their school, give back all the gear, and apologize. One of the biggest life lessons I've ever had.

—[Student quote]

One of the great joys in my life was to be able to teach and coach Pete and Brooke at Park View. Our family lived outside of the attendance area for the Patriots, but we were able to get special permission for them to attend PV. Pete played basketball and baseball, and I know he always had that self-imposed pressure to perform well so people wouldn't say he was playing because he was the coach's son. He was a good player who always got the best out of his natural ability.

Brooke played basketball and I gave up my basketball coaching for a while so I could attend her games and support her. She was also my manager in baseball, and she pretty much ran the show as she got older. I had an unspoken rule that no one could sit down during the game except the pitcher if he was tired. I wanted everyone up and supporting their teammates, either when we were at bat or in the field defensively.

I had a freshman on the Varsity who had a lot of potential, but he was not a starter and didn't see much action. We were playing at home one night, and he decided to sit on the ball bucket and watch from there. Brooke admonished him to get up and reminded him that no one sits. An inning or so later she sees him back on the bucket. She walked up to him and said, "I need to get a ball out of the bucket." When he got up Brooke took the bucket of balls and put them in the corner of the dugout! No one tried to sit on the ball bucket after that!

I knew we would have a good team in '84, even though we had only one senior. Two excellent pitchers, Ron Griffith and Randy Boyer, and a stud future NFL player behind the plate, Jeff Lageman, led a young team to the State Title game which was to be played at our field.

We were to play Abingdon, a team from southwest Virginia sporting a 21-1 record, on Saturday, June 2nd. They were making the long drive to Sterling on Friday to practice and then spend the night before the big game. On Thursday night, I got a call at my home in the evening from a man who identified himself as a reporter from the local Abingdon newspaper. He purported to ask about our team, but quickly switched to talking about how great the team from Abingdon was, that they had a shortstop who was going to play for UVA, etc. I didn't get to say much about my team before he ended the conversation.

We had finished practice the next day and I admonished my players not to stay and watch Abingdon practice, as I was worried about our guys getting psyched out. I was waiting at the field when their charter bus pulled up, carrying their four coaches and twenty-four players. As I walked up to meet their head coach, I immediately recognized his distinctive accent. It was the same as the "newspaper" reporter! He had called trying to psych me out.

You always worry about the mental state of high school players when things don't start out well, but after the top of the first inning I knew we would be alright. I had told our guys the key to the game would be keeping their leadoff hitter, a shortstop named Necessary, off of the bases. On the second pitch of the game, Necessary hit a home run off Randy. Coming into the dugout after getting the next three hitters out, Randy laughs and says, "Coach, I kept him off of the bases."

We went on to win the State Championship 6-4 before more than a thousand jubilant fans!

Glad I saw this as I'm not on Facebook much, but put a big smile on my face. Could write a book on the greatness of times we had with you, Mike Nunnally, as coach. We had more fun than anybody! Early season practices inside diving headfirst in the hallways conditioning (splitting my chin on one occasion with T-shirt that had a logo . . . it grabbed lol). Blocking tennis balls in catcher's gear on P.E. mats. List could go on forever. Had many practices and games in my life in my life and none have been better, more anticipated, or more joyous than PVHS baseball. Thanks coach! And oh . . . the state championship game at home down a couple runs late in the game and winning! Top of the list!"

—[Student quote]

When possible, I threw in a dose of humor in the classroom, gym, or outside during P.E. One of the most important lessons I learned early on in my career was to set the proper tone with the students in a new school year, as it is next to impossible to regain control of an unruly class. (Some old salts said don't smile before Christmas.) We were in Advanced P.E. class, and this young man was constantly opining about what we should be doing in class on any given day. I said to him, "When I want your opinion, I'll beat it out of you!"

Of course, we had a set curriculum to follow, and I usually adhered to it, as our class shared gym and field space with several other classes. I said it as a joke, but he got the message. I could be a hard ass if I wanted to, but I really considered myself as a benevolent dictator when teaching health or P.E.

Classroom management is a necessary component of good teaching. With a group of thirty to thirty-five students, a teacher has their hands full.

If I couldn't keep a certain amount of control, nothing positive could take place, and no learning would be the outcome.

I really hit my stride in 1984, the year I became director of St. George's Camp, a summer camp run by the Episcopal Diocese of Virginia. It was my staff at camp that really gave me some valuable lessons in dealing with both groups and individuals. The main learning for me was the ability to separate my feelings for the individual from their negative attitude or actions. "I like you; I just don't like what you are doing." Much easier said than done! Whenever I had a run-in with a student, I made sure to greet them in a positive way the next time I saw them. Showing them it was not personal.

I rarely sent a kid to the office, and then only for defiance. If I told someone to do something and they refused, then they had to go. No tardy slips. etc. for me. I handled my own problems. Tardy?: ten pushups, next time doubled, and so on. Girls and boys, I didn't discriminate. A girl would only be late once or twice, but once a guy hit three tardies, that was enough for him. Number four would be eighty pushups. Put your head down in health class? I would make the culprit stand up. I've yet to see a student fall asleep standing up.

These methods got the attention of the class and had an effect going forward. I found the students would respond to discipline in a positive way if I was fair, consistent, played no favorites, and didn't make it personal. Discipline was usually meted out with a smile. I learned how to get a large group's attention from my staff at camp. I would tell my students there was a zipper attached from their lips to their elbow, and that when they raised their hand, the mouth went shut. Then I told them that when I raised my hand, they were to raise theirs.

With a little practice, there was no reason for me to raise my voice to get their attention. I used to dismiss tables in the cafeteria after I had checked to make sure all the food and trash was cleaned up. I would raise my hand and wait until everyone got quiet, then do the dismissal. You would probably be shocked at how quick a group of more than four hundred teenagers could get quiet. They wanted to get out of there.

> So many. Hungry mongoose is a quick mongoose. When you caught me in 7-11 at fourteen buying dip and said, 'working on that lip?' It was a different time. Some of my best memories were from that team. You had the most impact on my life as a coach. You were tough, hard-nosed, demanding, yet understanding, soft to those that needed it. You knew what every person on your team needed. Which was suicides. LOL.
> —[Student quote]

One fall in my Advanced P.E. class, this funny incident occurred. There was always that one student, usually a guy, who just seemed to need everyone's attention, and would act out to get it. Well, the old coach was waiting for them. This one student acted out, and I told him to leave the gym, go outside and run to the Safeway truck. (This was an old Safeway truck that had been donated to the football team to hold equipment) I'd say it was close to a half mile out there and back.

When he returned after a few minutes, I asked, "Did you run all the way to the truck and back"?

He answered, "Yes sir." I knew immediately I had my man as his breathing had not changed.

A couple of days passed, and the same student acted out again, and I sent him to run to the truck and back. When he returned, I asked him if he had run to the truck, and his answer was, no surprise, "Yes." Again, no heavy breathing.

I surmised that he was leaving the gym and just hanging outside for a few minutes, and then jogged back into the gym. But I waited to set the trap. A guy like that couldn't help but brag that he had pulled one over on me, so all the other boys heard about it in the locker room.

A few classes later, he acted out again. (Why not, he probably thought? He gets to be the center of attention with really no repercussions.) I called his name, pointed, and told him to run to the truck. He comes back into the gym a few minutes later, and I asked, "Did you run to the truck?"

His answer, "Yes sir."

I saw a few of the boys in the class smiling, so I asked him again. Same answer. I motioned him to come over and said, "Let me see your arm." As he stuck it out, I grabbed his wrist with one hand, and started taking his pulse with my index and middle finger of my other hand. Slow and steady beat.

The class realized what I was doing, and they were flabbergasted! I'm sure they were thinking, you can't get away with anything with Chief. He knows all the tricks. We all had a good laugh, then went outside to watch the boy run to the truck and back three times. It took him a while, but he did it.

I always got along great with the kids who misbehaved or were on the fringe. Hell, I used to be one of them, so I understood them better. A little arm around the shoulder; a little TLC; and letting them know that someone was in their corner meant a lot to them.

> Most definitely the most I learned in high school
> was from you. I will respect and honor the time you
> gave me to make me what I am today. Thanks coach,
> more than you could ever imagine.
> —[Student quote]

If I ever thought I was in the wrong profession all those years, hearing from these and other former students and ballplayers lets me know I was the lucky one. My purpose in life was to work with and help others, and my early life showed me the importance of that calling.

When Elaine and I married in June of '73, it was at the Lutheran Church where Elaine and her family worshipped. We had wanted to be married in the beautiful St. James Episcopal Church in Leesburg, but the Rector, Jack Smith would not allow it since we had not been attending services there. That was disappointing, but we were living in Leesburg and decided to attend St. James anyway. Our son Pete ('77) and our daughter ('80) Brooke were both baptized there.

Here again, as with Church of the Ascension in Norfolk, and Emanual Episcopal in Covington, the Episcopal church was to play a huge role in my life.

SECTION FIVE
ST. GEORGE'S CAMP

Unchained

38

ALL WILL BE REVEALED

In the fall of 1983, I participated in a weekend retreat with the Vestry of St. James. We were spending the weekend at Shrine Mont, the Camps and Conference Center for the Episcopal Diocese of Virginia. The Vestry consists of twelve elected parishioners who support the mission of the church, select the rector, and manage the resources and finances of each individual parish. I believe this was my first time serving on the Vestry, and I had never visited Shrine Mont.

Rev. Jack Smith, our priest, gave us a brief history of Shrine Mont, a retreat and conference center in the town of Orkney Springs. It includes about eleven hundred acres of forest in the Great North Mountain in the Shenandoah Valley. Numerous cottages and the Virginia House, a four stories high former hotel built in 1873, give Shrine Mont a capacity of around six hundred guests. The large stone outdoor chapel is the Cathedral Shrine of the Transfiguration, which is the Cathedral for the Diocese of Virginia. The natural amphitheater was built in the woods, and very large rocks were placed to form an arch, a sacristy, and a bell tower. It was completed in 1925, and the current director of Shrine Mont, Wilmer Moomaw, helped in the construction at age fourteen.

We had some free time after lunch on Saturday, and Jack asked anybody who wanted to go on a hike to meet him outside. I decided to join the group, and as we wound our way up the hill to climb the stairs that led to a large wooden cross, we passed through a rustic group of wooden cabins. We spent a few minutes of silence at the cross, taking in God's beauty all around us, and praying in silence for whatever was on our hearts. I can't remember what I prayed for, but soon I was to be given the most precious gift!

On the way down from the cross we passed through the camp again, and Jack took us into this small cabin. He told us his family lived here in the summers from '70–'73, when he was the Director of St. George's Camp, a summer camp run by the Diocese. The cabin was very small, and I couldn't believe Jack lived here for eight weeks at a time with his wife Eleanor and three children.

It wasn't too long after that weekend that Jack and I shared lunch together and he told me the position of Director for St. George's was open, and he felt I would be a good fit. Did he set me up when he took us up there during the Vestry retreat? I don't know, but I'm glad he showed us the camp.

I talked it over with Elaine, and we thought it would be a good opportunity for our family. Pete was six, and Brooke was three, and we were sure they would have a good time. It didn't pay much, but we would be eating all our meals in a central dining hall, so no food shopping or cooking for Elaine. That was a big selling point. The only drawback was that camp would take up almost all our summer vacation.

I traveled to Fredericksburg for the interview with the Camps and Conferences Committee for the Diocese, and it wasn't long before I learned that we would be heading to camp! We invited Jack, Eleanor, and Sarah, their youngest daughter, over for dinner to learn more about what took place on "the mountain," as we would come to call it. We got some more encouraging information, but little did we know that our lives were going to be transformed forever by this experience.

Jack had told me that I would be working very closely with the priest who worked with all the camps. In the spring, a new priest was hired to follow the retired Churchill Gibson, and I invited him and his family to our house for dinner. Roger Bowen and his family were to become intertwined with the Nunnally family that first summer, and into the future right up to this day.

We had a pleasant meal and learned a bit about each other. Roger and Kennon had served in the Peace Corps for a few years, spending most of their time in Tonga, an island kingdom in the South Pacific. They were very close in age to Elaine and me, and had two younger kids, Tucker who was five, and Abby who was two, each a year younger than Pete and Brooke. Kennon was working at the National Cathedral's Beauvoir School and Rog was the Chaplain at the National Cathedral School for Boys in Washington, D.C. I thought we hit it off pretty well and looked forward to working with Rog.

1984 proved to be a banner year. In April, we moved from a subdivision in Leesburg to a house with three and a half acres in Broad Run Farms, near Sterling. We won that state championship in June, and started our first of nine summers at St. George's Camp.

School was out, and it was time to head to camp! Elaine and the kids were going to join me after staff training week. I was very excited to get up on the mountain with the fifteen camp counselors. I had met and hired them all over their Christmas break from college. Some I interviewed in Richmond, but the majority I was interviewing at VTS (Virginia Theological Seminary) in Alexandria, where Churchill Gibson lived and taught.

Churchill came from a long line of Episcopal priests and was a legend at St. George's, where he had been the chaplain for twenty years. He had agreed to be with me during the interviews, as he knew the counselors who were hoping to return and knew what to look for in the young people who were interviewing for the first time. When I called to verify his presence, he said he was sorry he was not feeling well. I had a feeling he just wanted me to get my feet on the ground by myself. It turns out the returning counselors and I were interviewing each other! I think they were concerned about having a coach become the director of what was a freewheeling, hippie-style, liberal church camp. In future years, Roger and I conducted the interviews together, as I valued his insights, different perspectives, and views.

I arrived a day early to meet with Jim Hasle, David Guthrie, and William "Yogi" Browning. Jim was to be my assistant director, David the camping director, and Yogi was to become my assistant director in the future. I liked these guys right away and was peppering them with questions about everything. I was in a job where I was learning everything from the young folks I was to lead. I trusted them immediately, and it wasn't long before I felt they trusted me.

The first order of business was to firm up the training schedule for the week, which included lots of role playing, worship, singing, cabin counselor duties, and staff bonding activities. It was going to be a busy week before the first campers arrived. I got some immediate respect from the guys when after dinner and some additional staff week work, they suggested we hit the pavilion for some hoops. I showed them that at the age of forty, I could still "ball"!

The Reverend Roger Bowen made it up on the mountain the following morning and was there with me to greet the entire staff as they arrived for the noonday meal. One of the first things I noticed as the staff greeted each other was that St. G.'s was a hugger's paradise! When the campers came a week later, one of the first things we did was to teach them the proper etiquette and technique for hugging St. G.'s style. Counselors would demonstrate in a humorous fashion the hugs that weren't cool: no side hugs, no A-frame hugs, no lingering hugs. The proper way was toes to toes, knees to knees, a quick embrace while greeting, and then on to the next.

Campers were not forced to hug, or made to feel like they had to, but most followed the lead of the counselors and their peers. In that time, as today, people need to feel that human touch in a non-threatening, loving way.

Later that day, after supper, we headed to the Shrine for worship, and I was immediately blown away by the music I heard! Several of the staff could play the guitar, and almost everyone had a very good voice. (Several of my former staff went on to become professional musicians.) It was a spirit-filled and uplifting service, with lots of fan favorites being requested from our very own rudimentary song books.

We closed this worship as we did so many with a prayer by Churchill Gibson, which to me embodies the very nature of Christianity. It is called the Shouting Prayer, and yes, it is always shouted.

> GOD LOVES THE WORLD
> GOD LOVES US
> GOD LOVES YOU
> I LOVE YOU
> GOD LOVES ME
> I LOVE ME
> THANKS BE TO GOD
> AMEN

After worship, it was off to the ballfield for evening games, following the schedule we would have when the first-session campers arrived. After a rousing game of ultimate frisbee, we all pulled out our sleeping bags and bedded down for the night in Lincoln Lodge, a community building named after the founder of St. George's Camp, Jim Lincoln.

The next morning after breakfast, we met the team of Wilderness Odyssey (WO), who would be working with us to build a low ropes course some distance up the trail near the Cross that I had visited with the Vestry and Jack Smith the previous fall. If you aren't familiar with a low ropes course, it is a challenging physical course that requires working together as a team with some level of skill and considerable determination. I'll explain more below.

WO was also part of the camps program for the Diocese, focusing on wilderness camping and team building. It was obvious from the start that these folks were professionals. As we gathered, they explained that we would be carrying all the materials we needed to build the ropes course up the mountain with us. That made sense to me, but what came next was a total surprise.

As they paired us up to carry the materials, they gave one of each pair some type of imaginary disadvantage. Examples included being deaf, not being able to speak, the use of only one arm, etc. They paired me, the oldest, with Henry Burt, the youngest counselor. Something must have clicked right away as Henry and I maintain a close friendship to this day.

I forget the exact number, but we built several "initiatives" or challenges on that first day. Two that come to mind immediately are the wall and the trust fall. The wall was probably about ten feet tall, with smooth boards making up the width of around eight feet. There was a narrow walkway attached near the top on the other side of the wall, so participants who had gotten over the wall could stand and reach down to help others get to the top. It took a lot of planning and cooperation to figure who had the ability to get over first, and then who would have the best chance being the last one over.

The trust fall is aptly named. A single participant would climb up to a log which was supported six to eight feet off the ground. The remainder of the group would form two lines below, facing each other shoulder to shoulder, positioned in such a way as to catch the camper who was on the log when they let themselves fall. The catchers would intertwine their extended arms so as to form a secure interlocking landing zone.

Here is the toughest part; the camper who is to fall has to have their back to the campers below, keep their arms crossed, and grab their shoulders. This prevents flailing arms hitting someone below. Let me tell you, falling this way on purpose is not a natural act! One additional instruction was key; arch your back so that your weight will be distributed evenly among the folks below. If you "butt dip," you may break through the arms and hit the ground. Every cabin was scheduled to do the ropes with a cabin of the opposite sex every session. This was a great team-building and confidence-boosting activity!

On some occasions, it took a long time to get the entire group through this as it could be scary for some. Naturally I was asked to go first when the build was completed. At six-foot-three and 210 pounds, I was a load, but they eventually talked me into falling!

I was increasingly impressed with the staff as the week unfolded. All of these young people were in college or headed that way in the fall. As a group, they were smart, talented, funny, quick-witted, irreverent in all the right ways, and seemed to sincerely love St. George's and its mission. I made it a point to get some one-on-one time with all of them during those times when we weren't all together. Roger and I also got to know each other better, and I came to appreciate and value his judgment as I watched him do his work.

As per the camp schedule, when the kids arrived, the staff was led in worship by Rog right after dinner. I could see right away that here was a self-assured man grounded in his faith. Quiet and softspoken by nature, Rog nevertheless commanded attention by his obvious sincerity and love of fellow man. He has a keen, discerning mind, and was a natural in counseling both staff and campers over the years.

I was learning a lot real quickly about what went on during the camp sessions, and at the same time we had to unpack stuff and clean the camp cabins and buildings. Lots of dirt and dust, as the cabins, lodges, and latrines were all screened, with no way to totally keep the elements out. We had rudimentary art supplies to organize and put away in Moomaw Lodge, camping packs and supplies went in Igor, and the sports equipment went in part of a storage building down the hill next to the ballfield. Igor was also the home for the summer of Dave Guthrie, the camping director, and Jim

Hasle, the assistant director. The screened-in back porch of Igor was also a staff hangout, particularly in the evening after lights out.

The staff training week was going along pretty much as planned when I got a big shock. Jim and Yogi came to see me, and it was like, "Houston, we have a problem!" It seems that one of the male staff, Brad, wanted to quit and head to Richmond to be with his girlfriend. What the hell? First off, I was incredulous. Was he really so lovesick that he couldn't be away from her for more than a few days at a time? There was always time off between sessions and Richmond was only a couple of hours away. What also frosted me was that he didn't have the guts to come and talk to me about it in person. I'm glad he showed his colors early though, as it would have been tough if he had quit the camp in mid-summer.

I didn't have time to get too upset about the situation though, as Jim and Yogi already had a pinch hitter in mind, Kirk Van Scoyoc. Kirk was a former counselor, and legendary Program Director and was twiddling his thumbs at home. He was available to step in. I'm pretty sure they had already spoken to Kirk by the time I called him. I explained the situation and let him know the position available was for that as a cabin counselor. He indicated that he was packed and ready to come to camp.

Kirk was by far the best pinch hitter I ever inserted into the line-up! The dude was killer on the banjo and had a great voice to boot. He stepped right in and played his part. I had hired Kristin Waskowicz to be the Program Director, and this was to be her first summer in that position. To my knowledge Kirk never stepped out of his lane, never second-guessed Kristin, or did anything but support her in this high-profile position.

It was the last day of staff training, and the first group of campers would be headed to the mountain the next day. I felt good about what we had accomplished. We had cleaned the camp, up, built the ropes course, focused on our "staff body," (more about that later) gone over the daily schedule, firmed up our worship outline with Rog, and established registration day responsibilities. It seemed to me that everyone was rested and focused on the job ahead.

We had planned to meet on the ballfield after dinner and worship for the "stroke circle." I had asked what that was all about, but I got the patented St. G.'s answer to most every question asked by a camper, "All will be revealed." I couldn't tell you the number of times over the years that I have used that phrase with my family, campers, students, or ballplayers.

St. G.'s was full of surprises that first summer, and I learned so much from my staff that I have carried with me ever since. The young people I worked with over the years were remarkable and taught me so much.

Unchained

39

STROKE CIRCLE

At the appointed time, we all sat in a circle facing each other, sitting closely side-by-side to make the group more intimate. After a short prayer came an explanation of the process, mainly for the new folk like Rog and me, and the first-year counselors. The idea was for everyone to say something positive, or something they liked about each person in the circle. Hence the word "stroke." No surface comments such as, "I like your hair," or "You are a good frisbee player," etc. The stroke was not meant to be superficial, but needed to carry some real weight behind it, with a short qualifying story or example. "You are a good listener," "I saw you showing empathy," or "You really put forth a good effort and stretched yourself when we built the ropes course." Those kinds of affirmations could lift a person up and show that they were appreciated and loved.

There were seventeen in the circle, so it was obvious this was going to take some time. (In one marathon stroke circle a few years later, it took six hours to finish! We named it "the miracle!" Got the T-shirt to prove it!)

They started with me! I was not ready in any way for what followed. Mike Nunnally does not cry! Mike Nunnally does not let his emotions get the better of him. That wall I had built up in my youth had softened a little, but I still kept that shell of protection in place and at the ready. As the counselors in the circle began to "stroke" me, looking at me eye to eye, I felt myself welling up inside, and by the time the last stroke was finished, I was bursting open.

They were saying these things about me? It was almost as if Christ was speaking through them to me. Yes, I WAS a good boy. My brain went numb, and I reached a point where I wasn't comprehending, but my heart and my soul were overflowing. As I received my last affirmation, overcome with emotion, I didn't know what to do, so I started doing forward rolls away from the group, tears rolling down my cheeks!

It did take a while to finish the whole group, but even today I count that experience as one of the most poignant and transforming three hours of my life!

Elaine showed up with the kids just about the time first session started, and luckily Kennon, Tucker and Abby were there also. It was tough on Elaine as she had to handle all of the parenting duties as I was totally immersed in my job. I participated in almost all the activities the camp offered that first summer, as I was trying to see how everything worked.

As that first summer went on, Elaine was able to involve Pete and Brooke in some of the activities, and they all bonded well with Kennon and her kids. Roger and I decided early on to go along with the camp program that first summer; to watch, learn, and then evaluate, making changes later as needed. Rog was mainly focused on worship, and he had his hands full with the three other camps going on that summer: music and drama camp, art camp, and Wilderness Odyssey.

When I did think we should make changes in future years, my goal was to have the staff initiate the change, or at least agree as a group. Case in point: Igor's back porch. As I've said before, it was used as a hangout for staff during the day but mostly after lights out for the camp. When I arrived, there was also a history of staff members drinking there. Obviously not cool—for a number of reasons! So we talked about that policy, and by the end of that summer, it was agreed by the staff that this was not appropriate going forward.

I found over the years that if the staff set staff and camp policy, they would be more likely to follow the policy, and also would hold each other accountable. My role in this regard was as someone who presented information and then facilitated the discussion around a particular issue. Doing this took time, and it would have been easier to just state a policy change. I saw one of my roles as counselor to the counselors, and I wanted them to grow in their ability to make thoughtful, mature decisions that affected others as well as themselves.

So, what was St. George's Camp all about? It was a church camp that offered a variety of activities that encompassed sports, field games, art, newspaper, swimming, hiking, canoeing, and of course worship with songs geared toward younger folks. Those aspects of camp were not that different from what you might find at similar Christian camps. Over the years though, a specific passage from the New Testament became the touchstone for St. G.'s and has come to be referred to as the "Body Passage."

Paul's first letter to the Corinthians, verses 12–27 (NIV).

[12]Just as a body, though one, has many parts, but all its many parts form one body, so it is with Christ. [13]For we were all baptized by[a] one Spirit so as to form one body—whether Jews or Gentiles, slave or free—and we were all given the one Spirit to drink.

[14]Even so the body is not made up of one part but of many. [15]Now if the foot should say, "Because I am not a hand, I do not belong to the body," it would not for that reason stop being part of the body. [16]And if the ear should say, "Because I am not an eye, I do not belong to the body," it would not for that reason stop being part of the body. [17]If the whole body were an eye, where would the sense of hearing be? If the whole body

were an ear, where would the sense of smell be? [18]But in fact God has placed the parts in the body, every one of them, just as he wanted them to be. [19]If they were all one part, where would the body be? [20]As it is, there are many parts, but one body.

[21]The eye cannot say to the hand, "I don't need you!" And the head cannot say to the feet, "I don't need you!" [22]On the contrary, those parts of the body that seem to be weaker are indispensable, [23]and the parts that we think are less honorable we treat with special honor. And the parts that are unpresentable are treated with special modesty, [24]while our presentable parts need no special treatment. But God has put the body together, giving greater honor to the parts that lacked it, [25]so that there should be no division in the body, but that its parts should have equal concern for each other. [26]If one part suffers, every part suffers with it; if one part is honored, every part rejoices with it.

[27]Now you are the body of Christ, and each one of you is a part of it.

This passage was just perfect for a large group of campers, as it says to them that each one is important, regardless of their differences. At the opening worship after supper on registration day, each camper was given a piece of string, most often some kind of camping tarp rope. The string represented them as an individual, a part of the "body" of camp, and was generally tied onto their wrist.

These "body strings" were to play a significant part in the life of the camp, as there was a challenge issued to each camper, each cabin, and the camp as a whole. The challenge was to bring everyone into the fold, to make everyone feel welcome, to treat all with respect and dignity. To help each other when needed and to leave no one out of any activity or part of camp life.

This challenge, along with worship, was the primary focus of St. George's Camp. All of the activities were used as a vehicle to strive toward this goal. Each day in staff meeting, there was time put aside for the staff to address how the camp was doing in this area, both in the individual cabins and the camp body as a whole. When the staff felt there had been significant growth in the camp in this area, there was a special worship service to celebrate. At this extremely high energy service, each camper untied their string and added it to the others to make a very large single rope of all the strings. We formed the rope into a necklace, similar to a Hawaiian lei, which was passed around from camper to camper, and staff to staff, with the goal of everyone wearing the "body strings" before the final worship

At the final worship to end camp with family and friends present, the individual strings were untied from the large rope and given to the campers to put back on their wrists to keep as a symbol of their time at camp. Of course, the chances of any camper getting the exact same piece of "body string" they wore initially was almost nil, but that was even better, as they had another camper's part of "the body," and they had been changed themselves by their time at camp

There were many tales told of family and friends searching for these "body strings" if they got misplaced, even at the bottom of a swimming pool!

There was one problem with the "body" theology as it had been put forth to the cam

As that first summer of camp drew to a close, I met with each member of the staff for a time of reflection and evaluation, and to discuss their potential plans for next summer. Some staff they knew their time at St. G.'s was over, but for others I learned to give them a little nudge out the door in a loving way. The majority of the staff was eager to return, depending on what role they would be asked to play. I had to orchestrate a delicate dance with these end of summer discussions about the future.

Over the years, there were only one or two staff members who were asked not to return, and I had to take equal share in their failure as counselors. Perhaps there was some cue I had missed during the interview process, or something I could have done during the summer to help them be successful. After the third summer however, many of them were former campers, and I had a pretty good idea about how they would perform in their job.

40

THE PROFESSOR

I always tried to hire at least one counselor every summer who was new to the mountain, one who had never been a camper, as they often brought new ideas, a new perspective, and new energy with them. After a couple of summers, Roger and I felt the need to add some diversity to the staff, and so we made the decision to intentionally interview some young people of color.

That fall we met and headed south down Interstate 95 to St Paul's College in Lawrenceville, Virginia, one of the Episcopal Church's several, historically black colleges. We had arranged for some publicity for our interviews and so we had a few young people already lined up and scheduled when we arrived on the campus. It was a fruitful day, as we ended up hiring two new staff for the upcoming summer.

The second interviewee was a young man named Larry Toomer. He came in for the interview dressed in a suit and tie and we noticed that he was a few years older than the normal college student. We were immediately impressed with his outgoing demeanor, his self-assurance, and basically everything about him. As we were talking, he told us that he helped a lot of the students at St. Paul's with their classwork and helped them study for tests. He said they had nicknamed him "the professor."

After the interview with each prospective counselor, Rog and I would take a few minutes to share our impressions, make notes, etc. Larry Toomer had made a big impression with both of us, and we were honestly questioning whether he was for real! When we called the next candidate in a few minutes later, the first question I asked was, "Do you know the young man who just walked out of here?" The young lady answered, "Yes, we call him the professor because he helps a lot of students here!" Obviously, in our minds he was immediately hired, and Fess (his nickname at camp) added so much to St. G.'s over the next two summers!

We also hired a female student to come as a counselor, but at the last minute she bowed out. Back to the list I went and hired a freshmen girl named Cheryl Kelly. Her father was a Baptist minister near Emporia, and I remember he dropped her off at eight p.m. the night before staff training was to begin. She was totally out of her element in the woods at first, but rallied and was a good cabin counselor for someone who had just turned seventeen!

I had never bothered to ask a college student how old they were! Fess was awesome in drag and Cheryl did a realistic version of Whoopi Goldberg to keep us entertained between sessions! Years later Fess would call me and ask about some of the games and activities we used, so I guess he continued working with young people.

It was year four at St. George's Camp and trouble was on the horizon! All systems were go heading into the summer of '87, and there was no indication on my part of what was to come. I felt that Rog and I had really hit our stride with the theology and mission of St. G.'s, and we had a great mix of talent, experience, and youth in the staff. There was palpable excitement around the Episcopal Diocese of Virginia regarding all the blossoming Shrine Mont Camps, and enrollment for the summer was up. At St. G.'s for example, we were going from three sessions to four, which I felt was a testament to what the entire staff had been doing for the past three summers.

Staff training week went well, and everyone knew that I would be missing the first week of camp. I was headed to California to meet Pete and Elaine after Pete's fourth ear operation. He was born with microtia of the right ear, which in his case meant there was an earlobe but no ear canal, etc. Obviously, this meant he had substantial hearing loss, and he had to learn to deal with that and the fact that his ear looked different from others. In a series of four operations, he had a portion of his rib cartilage removed, shaped like an ear, and grafted to his skull. In this way, his right ear would grow normally along with his head and all other parts of his body. The operations were done by a Dr. Burt Brent, who helped pioneer this technique. Everything went well and we were all in good spirits heading home and back to camp.

Unchained

41

"YOU ARE THE DEVIL"

When I got back on the mountain, the staff was buzzing about the man who had been placed in charge of camps for the summer. Bruce Newell and his wife, Ingrid, were going to be living among us as he took the reins overseeing all the camps on the mountain. Bruce was a former Admiral in the Navy, and at one time had commanded a nuclear submarine. He was studying at Virginia Theological Seminary with hopes of becoming a priest, and had been sent to Shrine Mont to oversee the summer camp program by our Bishop, Peter Lee. In addition, Bruce's wife, Ingrid, was given the job as camp nurse.

Bruce and Ingrid were not a good fit for several reasons. As an Admiral, Bruce was used to being the big show and having underlings kowtow to his every wish and command, regardless of whether they were good ideas or not. This kind of thinking was anathema at St. G.'s, where consensus ruled the day. Coming from a career in the military, he also wasn't used to some of the long-haired, laid back, sloppily dressed male staff. The main problem I saw though, was that Bruce would make snap judgments based on his very limited experience and was questioning things that had been proven to be successful over the years. Instead of talking to folks face-to-face, he often sent memos.

Ingrid was a nice lady but was out of her element with these young campers. It was obvious from the start that she hadn't been around young people for some time. She seemed to me to be a very uptight person, wanting everything to be perfect, including herself. There was always a lot of tension when they were around each other, and everyone else.

My assistant director William "Yogi" Browning was running the camp while I was in California. Yogi was great with kids, had the respect of the staff, and I had no doubts that he was up to the job! When Elaine, Pete, and I returned from California, Ingrid and Bruce were in a tizzy! On the previous Sunday, which was our "Easter" celebration at camp, they had taken the usual hike to the top of North Mountain. It could be a tough hike for any eight- and nine-year-olds who weren't used to physical activity, but one of the tenets of camp was to "stretch yourself."

Evidently it was a hot day in June, but the camp had a rest period when they got back. That evening a dance had been planned for evening program, and, as usual for first session, it was held in Lincoln Lodge up at the camp. During the dance, several kids got tired and had to sit down for a while. Evidently one camper was hyperventilating and was receiving a lot of attention as a result.

Now you probably didn't realize that hyperventilating is "contagious," but I have seen it happen at camp a few times over the years! Some campers want that special attention for themselves, and it's easy enough to start breathing rapidly. Hyperventilating is not dangerous to your physical health, and usually dissipates quickly. Ingrid panicked over this incident, and we were ordered to purchase extra coolers, to always carry water with us going forward, and to have planned water breaks during activities.

This was unnecessary as campers always had access to water, and as time went on, we resumed our normal operation. But the damage had been done. For the rest of the summer everyone on staff mistrusted Bruce and Ingrid, and shielded them from certain aspects of camp.

A couple of days later, Bruce was complaining about the staff at breakfast, and I told him I felt they were outstanding. I invited him to staff meeting before lunch to clear the air. He agreed to come as he handed me a memo with a list of ten or so things he wanted changed or done by five o'clock, or my job as director would be in jeopardy. It was all BS, and as far as I was concerned, he just wanted to see if I would jump through some hoops for him. It was another case of "Because I said so,"—and, by now, you know how I react to that!

I let some of the more veteran staff know some of what was in the note, and they were ready for him when he sat down at the staff meeting. To say the meeting was contentious would be an understatement, as the staff let him have it with both barrels! They weren't intimated in the least by his military credentials, and he was told he didn't know what the hell he was talking about regarding St. G.'s! I remember specifically Henry Burt, the program director, yelling at Bruce, "You are the devil!" He just sat there and took it.

I heard rumblings of some staff talking about quitting if I got fired, and I spread the word that this was not an option. Those campers who were headed to camp later that summer were counting on them. Elaine jumped in and spoke to Bruce telling him he was making a big mistake, and that he should wait a while before he made a rash decision.

I had crumpled up his demands and trashed them by the time dinner came around, ready for whatever came. He never said a word about it! There were no more issues the rest of the summer, and the Newells got into the flow and seemed to be having fun.

There was one funny incident involving Bruce and Henry. Staff who were going on a day off typically sat at the director's table during lunch, and Henry declared loudly that he was getting an earring when he went to Harrisonburg! Bruce told him he couldn't do that, so Henry showed up at breakfast the next morning with a ring in each ear!

Our staff was exceptional that summer, even handling an extra thirty fourth-session campers because of a scheduling quirk. After the final worship for fourth session, when the staff was cleaning the camp and putting away equipment until next summer, Bruce told me that he was wrong about the staff. He said he had worked for years with so many different talented people, but our staff was the hardest working group of people he had ever seen! The staff had a tradition of spending a few days together after camp, often at the beach, and Bruce handed me an envelope with several hundred dollars to give to them to spend on that "fifth session."

The Newells returned to their roles at Shrine Mont in the summer of '88 and they seemed to be our biggest fans. I never trusted Bruce after the incident the previous year, regardless of his words and cash at the end of that summer. He was soon to be the focus of much attention in the Episcopal Diocese of Virginia and beyond.

Here's a story that tells of a camper attending fourth session that summer of '88, that brought back into focus of our mission on the mountain and made all the uncertainty and trouble with Bruce Newell fade quickly away.

Patrick's raw emotions finally came out, and he was crying and hugging everyone in sight! I had noticed him right away in the registration line for St. George's Camp Session IV, sometime in the late 1980s. As the Director of St. G.'s, it was my job to notice everything. Patrick was a tall, gangly fifteen-year-old, and as he stood in line watching what was going on around him, his eyes were darting to and fro, and his body language was saying, "What the hell have I gotten myself into"? He was surrounded by the ninety or so campers, their parents and siblings, almost all of them very familiar with the camp and each other, and all of them excited for what lay ahead.

Session IV was for fourteen- and fifteen-year-old boys and girls, and many had been coming to camp for years, some since the age of eight. For the fifteen-year-olds it was their last summer to be at St. G.'s, and they wanted it to be the best session ever!

As I welcomed and worked the crowd, I made sure to introduce myself to Patrick and his sponsor, and made an attempt to put him at ease. Miserable fail! After registration, the campers headed up the hill to the camp and got settled into their cabins, home for the next thirteen days. Then it was off to the pool for a camp swim.

At the pool, I noticed Patrick staying off to the side, keeping to himself. It could be very intimidating for a "newbie" to be thrust into the big, raucous crowd of campers and counselors that made up the St. G.'s "body." His counselor was trying his best to engage Patrick and get him into the pool, and finally he jumped in and joined the crowd. After the swim, it was back up to camp to change, and then back down the hill for dinner.

The dining hall was usually very loud, but even more so for the first meal of Session IV. The campers were so excited to be back on the Mountain. At the end of the meal it was time for Announcements, and Henry Burt, the Program Director, got it started with his announcement song, the theme from the Johnny Carson Show. Everyone hummed the song loudly, (most knew it by heart) and then at the end screamed, "Heeeeere's Henry!" Henry announced it was up to the Shrine for worship, to the ball field for evening games, up to the camp for canteen, and then time for evening program", which was, "All Will Be Revealed!"

Now worship at St. G.'s was almost always a raucous and rowdy affair, with lots of guitars, singing, clapping, foot stomping, etc. The vast majority of campers knew the songs by heart, so you could hear our voices from quite a distance. As I was usually up front with the musicians and our chaplain, Roger, I had a good vantage point to observe the whole camp. I searched for Patrick, and noticed that he was standing with his cabin, arms crossed, and not participating. This was not unusual for a first-time camper as the whole scene could be very intimidating.

After worship, we headed over to the ball field for evening games, and the first order of business was a humorous skit about how to "Pass the Peace" at St. G.'s. Which meant hugging each other instead of shaking hands like the campers would have seen in their home churches. As explained earlier, we taught the "proper form" for hugging: No A-frame hugs, no side hugs, no arm hugs, no lingering hugs! It was: toes to toes, knees to knees, a quick embrace to say, "Peace be with you," and then move on to the next person.

Passing the peace at St. George's took a while, as the goal was to "peace" every other person in the camp, typically over a hundred folks! Although this hugging was encouraged, no one was forced to participate or ostracized for declining to hug someone else. Usually, this age group was all about it!

Patrick was having none of it and wouldn't let anyone even touch him. Again, not that unusual for someone in his situation. After the Passing the Peace, the campers headed up to the camp for canteen (sodas), then into Lincoln Lodge for evening program. Humorous "Rules Skits" were put on by the staff to go over the basic rules of camp. Just getting silly with the everyday do's and don'ts. It gave the rock stars, the counselors, a chance to shine, and the first-year counselors got a chance to introduce themselves to the whole camp in an informal way. (First year staff were often intimidated by the whole scene too!).

Then it was my turn to go over the "serious" rules for living together in community for the next thirteen days. No "camp couples," no PDA (public displays of affection), honor everyone's personal space, no smoking, no phone calls, etc. Then it was time for everyone to hit the latrines and go to their cabins.

After the "lights out" bell, I headed down to the Director's cabin with Elaine, Pete, and Brooke. Registration Day was a long day, and I was happy to relax a bit and talk about the day with Elaine.

My rest was short lived however. Soon a knock came on the door and Patrick's counselor asked me to step out onto our screened in porch. Patrick was with him and Patrick was livid. He demanded to go home! He said that he was a smoker, and no one told him he couldn't smoke at camp. I realized that probably wasn't the only reason he wanted to leave as he seemed like a fish out of water at St. G.'s.

In my mind the worst thing I ever had to do as Director was to send someone home, even if they were sick or injured. In my nine years at camp, I don't think I sent more than a handful of camper's home. So, what to do with Patrick? It was obvious to me that he needed to be at camp, and equally as important, the camp needed him! We all had so much to gain by the presence of this troubled young man.

I sent the counselor back to his cabin and asked Patrick to sit with me on the porch. I told him I understood the smoking thing as I had started smoking at an early age at Boys Home where I grew up. He started calming down a bit as we talked, and I asked him about his life in Richmond. Patrick said he was from a broken family and had been shuffled back and forth. He said he spent a lot of time on the streets. it was when I told him I had been a foster child for a while and briefly told him my story that the connection between us was made. He said he didn't go to church, so I surmised he got to St. George's through a concerned adult who was familiar with the camp.

I desperately wanted Patrick to stay for the full camp experience, and, while we were talking, a plan began to take shape in my mind. I let him know that I felt staying would be a great experience for him, and that the camp would be greatly diminished without his presence. I told him to give it a try for a couple of days, and then if he insisted on going home, I would give my permission.

I felt sure that forty-eight hours in this inclusive, fun, loving, caring Christian environment would win him over. I asked him how many cigarettes he had with him, and he said just half a pack, that he was planning on buying more at a store here. Patrick said he had his smokes on him, so I said, "Here's the deal, give me your cigarettes, then you and I walk outside, you smoke one last cigarette, and give camp a try for two days. He went for it! It took him a long time to smoke that cig to the end, then he walked back up to his cabin.

The next day during staff meeting I told everyone that Patrick was going to need extra love and attention, and to give him a little leeway when he needed it. As it turned out, the whole camp "body"(part of the Body of Christ) also realized what Patrick needed and welcomed him in with open arms! He gradually lowered his wall of self-protection and, after a few days, was having a blast! I made sure to check in and spend some time with Patrick almost every day, just to see how things were going for him.

Three nights before it was time for camp to end, we had an especially moving Christmas service in the outdoor shrine. It was a twilight service, at the end of a special day. As was our custom, we didn't pass the peace during the service because it was easier to go to the adjacent ball field to give space and time to close out the worship. The streetwise boy who wouldn't let anyone touch him ten days earlier was crying and hugging everyone in sight! I waited until he finished, then got my hug, letting him know how much it meant to me to have him stay. It was a good, long, teary-eyed hug for both of us.

Soon it was Final Worship for Session IV, the cars were rolling down Orkney Grade with some very excited, tired campers heading for home. The Spirit was alive and well on the mountain!

Every now and again Patrick would come into my mind, and I would wonder how he was doing. Then out of the blue, five years after his summer at camp, he wrote me a letter! It started out "You probably don't remember me . . ." Patrick said he was still in Richmond, and said he was doing well. He said he still didn't go to church, but he wanted to let me know that those thirteen days at St. George's had a profound influence on his life. Patrick said the love that was shown to him and others opened his eyes to the possibilities for his life.

Patrick, of course I remembered you, you added so much to our summer! Godspeed my friend! During my time as a teacher, coach, and camp director, I always had a special affinity for those on the edge, troubled youth. Hell, I knew exactly where they were at. I had been there myself!

The Nunnallys and Bowens shared our sixth and final year on the mountain together in '89, as after that summer, Rog took a new position as Head of School at the York School in Monterey, California. Our families had only grown closer over the preceding summers, and we bought a little country house together in the village of Orkney Springs, where Shrine Mont was located. In addition, we had spent a week together for several years at the beach in North Carolina immediately following camp.

It was a magical summer, culminated by a live recording in the small chapel of some of our favorite camp songs. The staff was jam packed with talented musicians, and even though everyone was bone tired, and ready to go home the last day of staff clean-up, we sang our hearts out! We had one boom mic and sang no retakes, but with the crickets singing loudly in rhythm in the background, we nailed it!

Check out "St. G.'s Live 1989 St. George's Camp Shrine Mont" on YouTube!

Unchained

254

42

ADJUST AND MOVE ON

I've got to tell you, the summer of '90 without my brother Rog around was a struggle at times. I missed his quiet, self-assured demeanor, his sage advice, his interaction and counseling with the staff, and our close friendship.

For the most part we fell into a pattern of having a different priest for each session, which posed a lot of challenges and took a lot of energy from everyone. The first order of business was to bring them up to speed on the theology of our camp, including the "body passage" and strings. Of course, they were also in charge of worship planning and implementation with each cabin, and the special worships of opening worship, Christmas, Easter, and Final Worship. It was a lot for them to absorb, and we learned to keep a staff member close by the priests during worship to prompt them if necessary. The best thing about the situation was that it kept our purpose and theology front and center among the staff the entire summer.

Without exception, the "priests of the session" were blown away by what was happening at St. G.'s. Nothing like this was taking place in any parishes around the Diocese, and it gave them a shot in the arm of the Spirit to take off the mountain with them.

By the end of the summer of '91, I found I was not looking forward to every event during a session, and I felt my time was coming to turn over the reins to someone else. I debated with myself and talked with Elaine, and our

Pete and Brooke, who were still campers themselves, and decided to give it one more summer and go out with a roar!

I was determined to go out the way I came in—enthusiastic and energetic about everything camp. For the most part, I did just that, and St. G.'s was aided by the addition for the summer of an excellent priest, Reverend Patrick Augustine. He got the fever right away, and with his deep booming voice praying "Abba Father," the staff and campers rallied to his call.

The summer wore on with the usual highs and lows, but soon Ryan Hopkins (Hopper) would need all our prayers and love. Ryan had been a "lifer" at St. George's, starting camp at an early age from his hometown of Ashland, Virginia. Or as Hopper would call it, the center of the universe. He had a big personality, was good looking, athletic, and a leader among his peers in his camper days. I distinctly remember his last session as a camper at age fifteen. Ryan came to camp playing the Mr. Cool role, acting as if the camp traditions and fourth session campers were beneath him. He was too mature and had mentally and emotionally moved on. Or so he thought.

Our special observance of Christmas in summer normally fell a couple of days before the end of camp. The "Christmas Eve" service took place in the beautiful outdoor stone shrine. It was a very moving and emotional time. The campers had just read "stroke sheets" from their parents in their cabins, and as they quietly made their way to worship, the shrine was filled with the magical light of candles and the eternal sounds of Gregorian chants echoing through the trees.

We sang the traditional Christmas hymns, which when played by acoustic guitars have a soft, soothing effect. The sermon was always the same, and veteran campers knew what was coming. The reading was a story out of *The Way of the Wolf* by Martin Bell, with a touching musical accompaniment.

"Barrington Bunny" is a tale of a small bunny with no family of his own, and he is cold, alone, and sad on this snowy Christmas Eve. A mysterious silver wolf appears and tells him two things: First, it is a gift to be warm, furry, and able to hop. "A free gift, with no strings attached." And second, the wolf tells him he is not alone, because "all of the animals in the forest are your family." Barrington then takes a small gift to the squirrels and beavers, saying, "Here is a gift, a free gift, with no strings attached." From "a member of your family."

Barrington sees a very small field mice who is lost from his family, and Barrington hops to him and covers the little fellow with his warm furry body. The field mice find their lost family member the next morning under Barrington's cold, frozen body. The great silver wolf comes and stays with Barrington all of Christmas day. (This is a modern-day parable about Christmas and Easter. God sends Jesus to us in love, and Jesus is sacrificed for us for the same reason.)

There were often tears shed as this story was read, even among the older campers who knew the story well. Now some folks might say it's wrong for young people to hear about the bunny's sacrifice and death, that it makes them sad. To that I say all Christians read and hear about Jesus' death and this, like all parables, is an easy to grasp analogy. After the service, as was our custom, we went to the ballfield to pass the peace, and we are all trying to make sure we give everyone a hug, which can be difficult in the near darkness. I had no trouble finding Ryan to hug, as he was bawling his eyes out! It had finally hit the cool guy that this was the end of his time for the magic of St. G.'s. I stayed with him for a while, wrapping him in my patented bear hug.

Later, Hopper returned as a cabin counselor and was still a leader among his peers. He was having a terrific summer. He and I got along great, and it was more like I was his friend who also just happened to be his boss. I got a call from his mom and dad with some horrific news they wanted to share over the phone with Ryan. They wanted me to be there in the director's cabin when he learned that his best friend, Tad, who was like a brother to him, had been killed in an automobile accident. This time his sobs cut me to the quick as I engulfed him. We sat and talked about his friendship with that young man, and neither of us had the answer to "why"? It was the hardest thing I ever had to do while at St. George's. The staff rallied around their friend who was hurting big time, but I'm sure it took a long time for Ryan to get over that nightmare of a loss.

Our capacity at St. G.'s was ninety campers, nine to a cabin, ten cabins. My last fourth session had ninety-five campers, as I just didn't want to turn anyone away. I think we triple-bunked the extra five, and the camper on that top bunk had to be careful not to hit their head on the rafters! I was trying to soak it all in one last time, while at the same time reminiscing over the past nine summers.

Those summers had changed my life in so many good ways and brought so much joy into my heart. I found myself tearing up at times as I realized how special the everyday flow of camp was to me. Just stepping back and watching the camp like a visitor at meals, evening games, worship, evening program, brought a fresh perspective. I was filled with delight and amazement as I watched the staff work their magic.

The only downside to these last few days was that Elaine and Pete were not there to share them with me. Elaine was painting watercolors in Monet's Garden in Giverny, France, and Pete was with her deadheading the flowers. So, it was just twelve-year-old Brooke and me feeling the last of the St. George's vibes. Before I knew it, it was Christmas, the last camp dance, Coffeehouse, and Final Worship. That last full-day former staff began to trickle in and there were hugs, laughter, and tears as we reminisced about the days gone by. I was drained by the end of the day but found enough energy to spend some quiet with my assistant director, Rad Burt. We talked about all the good times we had shared together during his six years on staff.

The next morning was a blur as more former staff showed up to help celebrate my nine summers as director, but it was also the last rodeo for those fifteen-year-old campers, and we had to make sure and give them a great sendoff also. The traditional slideshow was a raucous affair, and then it was time for worship.

The Shrine was packed with the campers, staff, friends, and families, and the fifteen or so former staff who came to see me off. That boy who had learned to hide all of his emotions was somewhere in my past, and the man who, over time, replaced him was getting all the feels, wave after wave! I pretty much lost it when the body strings were untied and passed out, and someone tied that last one to my wrist!

It was announced that Bishop Peter Lee of the Episcopal Diocese of Virginia had designated a scholarship in my name be given to one Boys Home Boy to come to St. George's every summer. The greatest honor and gift I have ever received.

Unchained

EPILOGUE

It's July 4, 2023, and I'm still here! I just got back from our house in Orkney Springs, which we still own with the Bowen family. I joined Brooke and her family, The Breddie Bunch: Brooke, Eddie, August (eight), and DeDe (five), as they put August into St. G.'s for the first time. Elaine was there also, and although we have been divorced for a few years now, we are good friends and continue to support our family in every way. Father Pete, our son, arrived the next afternoon after leading his Episcopal Wilderness Church service in Fletcher's Cove, Washington, D.C. We had a couple of nights around the campfire reminiscing about the good old days at St. George's with former campers, counselors, and friends.

I continued teaching and coaching at Park View High School until my retirement in December 2002. I was only fifty-nine, but I had given all I could in that profession and was pretty well burned out. I stayed active at St. James Leesburg, including leading a mission trip in 1995 to the Lakota Sioux Pine Ridge Indian Reservation in South Dakota. I did a little TV stint with a local cable company in Loudoun County, talking with coaches and athletes about their exploits.

Hurricane Katrina hit New Orleans very hard in August of 2005, and a couple of years later, St. James began mission trips to help rebuild the houses devastated by that terrible storm. I was lucky enough to be able to participate in all eleven trips, and led the last nine, as we went from gutting houses to rebuilding for those without flood insurance.

I fell in love with New Orleans and moved there in 2011 for three years. I loved every minute of it, especially my last two years living in the French Quarter! I found out my brain still worked, as I had to pass a test to become a certified tour guide. I started my own one-man shop and gave tours to families, couples, and people who knew each other. I wasn't interested in having a lot of folks at one time, I wanted to get to know my clients on a personal level.

I made a lot of new friends while in New Orleans, and dated a few nice ladies, but I didn't let myself get too involved as I knew I would head back to Virginia at some point to be near Pete and Brooke. When I did move back north it was to Richmond, and I spent a joyous year living with Pete just before he started attending Virginia Theological Seminary to become a priest.

Then it was back to Sterling, living with the Breddie Bunch until the time of COVID. I'm closing this out from my apartment about ten minutes from where they live in our old neighborhood of Broad Run Farms.

In the fall of 2018, I got a call from my old Greene Cottage buddy Donnie Wheatley, who was nearing the end of his time as the Executive Director at Boys Home. Donnie asked me to come up and give a basketball clinic for a week. Of course I said yes, and put the boys through their paces, and I think it surprised both the boys and myself that we had a good time together.

Near the end of the clinic, Donnie asked me to coach the team for the upcoming hoops season! That's how I became the oldest high school coach in Virginia for a couple of seasons! I moved up to "The Hill" in late fall, and it just so happened there was a spot open in Jack Gordon Cottage where the houseparent used to stay. Several older boys were living across the hall in the cottage, and I got to know them pretty well as the season went on.

I had a great two years there before COVID hit. It took a year for the guys to get used to a "professional" coach, and I think we went through nearly eighteen players during the course of the season, finishing with eight players and a losing record. The next winter was a different story though, as we finished 13-4 before COVID hit and took away our chance at the season-ending tournament. What a thrill for me though, to come back home at age seventy-seven and be a Boys Home Boy again!

I don't know what the future holds, but I know I have been a blessed man during my lifetime. Yes, it started out pretty tough, but God has always protected me and placed Angels in my path to help guide me along the way.

This book is dedicated to all those Angels, and to those friends, students, ballplayers, campers, and counselors who have supported me and enriched my life by their presence!

And of course to my family, who continues to be my strength and shield! God bless you all!

Unchained

AFTERWORD

This will be a personal note—because being in relationship with Mike is an individual and deeply personal experience. I was a nervous 18-year-old kid when I met Mike in the summer of 1984, having landed the only job I'd ever wanted—counselor at St. George's Camp. We were an unlikely friendship—Mike was an athlete, a father and husband, and a coach. I was decidedly not an athlete, a middling musician, and an irrepressible smart-aleck. Yet that summer began a friendship—and mentorship—that lasts to this day. Mike and I found common ground in our senses of humor and we share (to this day) a lasting devotion to the work of St. George's Camp.

Mike was my first mentor. As I have moved along in my career over the last three decades into roles where I have been called to lead larger and larger teams of people, first at the Diocese of Virginia and then at a large law firm, I've been asked many times what formed my leadership principles and style. My answer always starts with the lessons I learned from working side-by-side with Mike for five summers, and from the continued connection over the years. Mike coached baseball—a sport I've come to love—and he brought that coach's heart to his work at St. George's. He taught me that a great team needs a wide variety of folks with very different skills, and there is value in every single one of those teammates (even if it comes time for them to leave the team). The passage in Corinthians is the theological statement of what a team must be—to honor all, to care for all, to understand joy and pain is shared by all. Mike inculcated this understanding in many, many of us fortunate enough to work with him at camp.

Mike's story is not one that shows that sometimes the ordinary becomes extraordinary. It shows us that in the ordinary there is always something extraordinary. And if we look hard enough and engage in relationship, we may discover that both in others and in ourselves. It was a privilege to work for Mike, it has been a gift to have him as a guide in my head and heart throughout the years, and it is a tremendous blessing to now hear his whole story.

Mike will tell you that I often (always?) want to get in the last word. I am deeply honored he granted me the privilege here, with a phrase Mike used to end our staff meetings over many summers:

"...and there you have it."

Henry D.W. Burt
Richmond, Virginia
September 17, 2023

Made in the USA
Middletown, DE
11 October 2023

40546478R00157